James T. Sears, PhD
Editor

Gay, Lesbian,
and Transgender Issues
in Education
Programs, Policies,
and Practices

Pre-publication
REVIEWS,
COMMENTARIES,
EVALUATIONS . . .

"The book's richness comes from its diverse contributors: educators, students, and advocates from a wide range of geographic and racial backgrounds; and from its diverse approaches: theory and practice, statistics, policy, and personal narrative. Yet along with its remarkable inclusivity, *Gay, Lesbian, and Transgender Issues in Education* never loses sight of the most important focus of all—the students who move through our classrooms and schools. Like its host, the *Journal of Gay & Lesbian Issues in Education,* this book calls on us all to listen, to understand, and to act."

Rita M. Kissen, PhD
Associate Professor of Teacher Education,
University of Southern Maine

"International in scope, *Gay, Lesbian, and Transgender Issues in Education* takes a comparative approach to educational practices and policies for lesbian, gay, bisexual, transgender, and queer topics in countries such as Japan, China, Australia, New Zealand, the United States, and Canada. It addresses key issues, including school bullying, the roles of gay-straight alliances, the needs of transgender college students, and the problem of youth HIV infection, and it connects a focus on sexual identity with ethnicity, race, and socioeconomic class.

Drawn from personal narratives and from scholarship by some of our leading educational researchers, this rich and varied anthology adds a multicultural perspective to LGBT/Queer studies and helps solidify a place for LGBT/Queer perspectives in multicultural studies."

Warren J. Blumenfeld, EdD
Assistant Professor,
Multicultural and International
Curriculum Studies,
Department of Curriculum and Instruction,
Iowa State University

More pre-publication
REVIEWS, COMMENTARIES, EVALUATIONS . . .

"*Gay, Lesbian, and Transgender Issues in Education: Programs, Policies, and Practices* is a wonderful compilation of some of the best writing to appear in Volume One of the *Journal of Gay & Lesbian Issues in Education*. Skillfully edited by James T. Sears, PhD, the chapters in this book provide a global view of the state of affairs for lesbian, gay, bisexual, transgender, and questioning (LGBTQ) youth as they seek their education.

Many of the chapters offer first-person accounts of the struggles young people face in trying to attain their educational goals in schools in which harassment, intimidation, and violence are still rampant. The book also offers strategies for improving these school systems by employing some of the most creative and innovative practices in place in the United States and around the world. This book is a must-read for education professionals and anyone interested in improving the school experience for LGBTQ young people."

Craig Bowman
Executive Director,
National Youth Advocacy Coalition,
Washington, DC

HPP

Harrington Park Press®
An Imprint of The Haworth Press, Inc.
New York • London • Oxford

NOTES FOR PROFESSIONAL LIBRARIANS
AND LIBRARY USERS

This book is published by Harrington Park Press®, an imprint of The Haworth Press, Inc.

CONSERVATION AND PRESERVATION NOTES

All books published by The Haworth Press, Inc. and its imprints are printed on certified pH neutral, acid-free book grade paper. This paper meets the minimum requirements of American National Standard for Information Sciences-Permanence of Paper for Printed Material, ANSI Z39.48-1984.

Gay, Lesbian, and Transgender Issues in Education

Programs, Policies, and Practices

HARRINGTON PARK PRESS

Haworth Series in GLBT Community & Youth Studies
James T. Sears
Senior Editor

The Tomcat Chronicles: Erotic Adventures of a Gay Liberation Pioneer by Jack Nichols

Gay, Lesbian, and Transgender Issues in Education: Programs, Policies, and Practices edited by James T. Sears

Other Titles of Related Interest

Coming Out of the Classroom Closet: Gay and Lesbian Students, Teachers, and Curricula edited by Karen M. Harbeck

School Experiences of Gay and Lesbian Youth: The Invisible Minority edited by Mary B. Harris

Queer Kids: The Challenges and Promise for Lesbian, Gay, and Bisexual Youth by Robert E. Owens Jr.

In Your Face: Stories from the Lives of Queer Youth by Mary L. Gray

Social Services with Transgendered Youth edited by Gerald P. Mallon

Being Gay and Lesbian in a Catholic High School: Beyond the Uniform by Michael J. S. Maher Jr.

From Here to Diversity: The Social Impact of Lesbian and Gay Issues in Education in Australia and New Zealand edited by Kerry H. Robinson, Jude Irwin, and Tania Ferfolja

How Homophobia Hurts Children: Nurturing Diversity at Home, at School, and in the Community by Jean M. Baker

Addressing Homophobia and Heterosexism on College Campuses edited by Elizabeth P. Cramer

Straight Talk About Gays in the Workplace: Creating an Inclusive, Productive Environment for Everyone in Your Organization, Third Edition by Liz Winfeld

Gay, Lesbian, and Transgender Issues in Education

Programs, Policies, and Practices

James T. Sears, PhD
Editor

HPP

Harrington Park Press®
An Imprint of The Haworth Press, Inc.
New York • London • Oxford

371.826
Gay

For more information on this book or to order, visit
http://www.haworthpress.com/store/product.asp?sku=5180

or call 1-800-HAWORTH (800-429-6784) in the United States and Canada
or (607) 722-5857 outside the United States and Canada

or contact orders@HaworthPress.com

Published by

Harrington Park Press®, an imprint of The Haworth Press, Inc., 10 Alice Street, Binghamton, NY 13904-1580.

This book is a compilation of articles that appeared previously in the *Journal of Gay & Lesbian Issues in Education*, 1(1) (2003): 33-71; 1(2) (2003): 29-58, 77-87; 1(3) (2004): 7-22, 37-66; 1(4) (2004): 3-36, 41-60, published by The Haworth Press, Inc.

PUBLISHER'S NOTE
Identities and circumstances of individuals discussed in this book have been changed to protect confidentiality.

Cover design by Lora Wiggins.

Library of Congress Cataloging-in-Publication Data

Gay, lesbian, and transgender issues in education : programs, policies, and practices / James T. Sears, editor.
      p. cm.
"This book is a compilation of articles that appeared previously in the Journal of gay & lesbian issues in education, 1(1) (2003): 33-71; 1(2) (2003): 29-58, 77-87; 1(3) (2004): 7-22, 37-66; 1(4) (2004): 3-36, 41-60"—T.p. verso.
Includes bibliographical references and index.
      ISBN 1-56023-523-3 (hard : alk. paper) — ISBN 1-56023-524-1 (soft : alk. paper)
      1. Homosexuality and education. 2. Sexual minorities—Education. 3. Gender identity. I. Sears, James T. (James Thomas), 1951- II. Journal of gay & lesbian issues in education.
LC192.6.G38 2005
371.826'6—dc22
                                                                                          2004026628

CONTENTS

SECTION II: RESEARCH AND POLICY

ABOUT THE EDITOR

James T. Sears, PhD, specializes in research in lesbian, gay, bisexual, and transgender issues in education, curriculum studies, and queer history. He earned an undergraduate degree in history from Southern Illinois University, a graduate degree in political science from the University of Wisconsin, and his doctorate in education and sociology from Indiana University, which awarded him its Outstanding Alumni Award. Dr. Sears is the editor of the *Journal of Gay & Lesbian Issues in Education,* editor of the Haworth Series in GLBT Community and Youth Studies, and an award-winning author or editor of fifteen books. He has taught at Trinity University, Indiana University, Harvard University, Penn State, College of Charleston, and the University of South Carolina. He has also been a Research Fellow at the Center for Feminist Studies at the University of Southern California, a Fulbright Senior Research Southeast Asia Scholar, and a consultant for the J. Paul Getty Center for Education and the Arts. Additional biographical information can be found in *Who's Who in America.*

CONTRIBUTORS

Brett Beemyn earned a PhD in African-American studies and master's degrees in African-American studies, American studies, and higher education administration. Before becoming the GLBT student services coordinator at The Ohio State University, he was a faculty member at several different universities, teaching courses in African-American studies and lesbian, gay, bisexual, and transgender studies. Brett has edited or co-edited a number of texts, including *Bisexuality in the Lives of Men: Facts and Fictions* (2001); *Bisexual Men in Culture and Society* (2001); *Creating a Place for Ourselves: Lesbian, Gay, and Bisexual Community Histories* (1997); and *Queer Studies: A Lesbian, Gay, Bisexual, and Transgender Anthology* (1996). E-mail: <beemyn.1@osu.edu>.

Chad Beyer has advocated for social justice as an educator, nonprofit leader, and consultant for more than a decade. His areas of interest are democratization and sustainability in workplaces, schools, and other community organizations. He currently serves as executive director of the Gay, Lesbian, Bisexual, and Transgender Community Center of Utah. E-mail: <cbeyer@glccu.org>.

P. Jayne Bopp is the Program Against Violence project coordinator in the Women's Center, University of Hawaii at Manoa, Honolulu, Hawaii. She holds a master's degree in public health, specializing in maternal and child health and health education. She has more than fifteen years of experience implementing behavioral risk reduction programs with marginalized populations. She is also the board president of Harm Reduction Hawaii. E-mail: <pbopp@hawaii.edu>.

Rachel Bromley has a BA in English and gender studies and is working toward a master's degree (app) in social work at University of Canterbury, New Zealand. She is interested in working with GLBT students in some area of social services when she graduates. E-mail: <rcb27@student.canterbury.ac.nz>.

Sean Cahill, PhD, directs the Policy Institute of the National Gay and Lesbian Task Force. He is co-author of *Education Policy Issues Affecting Lesbian, Gay, Bisexual and Transgender Youth,* forthcoming from the University of Michigan Press. He is author of *Same-Sex Marriage in the United States: Focus on the Facts,* published in 2004 by Lexington Books. E-mail: <scahill@thetaskforce.org>.

Cloudia W. Charters is an author and consultant residing in Honolulu, Hawaii. E-mail: <cloudiacharters@msn.com>.

Peter Dankmeijer was trained as a teacher, but works now as a senior consultant on gay and lesbian issues. He is the director of Empowerment Lifestyle Services <www.empower-ls.com>, a nonprofit company that focuses on gay and lesbian emancipation in schools. In the Netherlands, he develops resources and implementation projects, advises authorities and nongovernment organizations, and trains teachers and volunteer educators. He is editor of the Dutch e-mail magazine "Feit and Vooroordeel" for diversity educators. His international activities include the coordination of the LGBT Education Network <www.lgbt-education.info>. E-mail: <info@empower-ls. com>.

Rodge Q. Fann is originally from mainland China and is currently a PhD candidate at New Jersey Institute of Technology. He serves as an assistant editor for the *Journal of Gay and Lesbian Issues in Education.* His other work includes two entries about LGBT in China for *[Homo]Sexualities, Education and Youth: An Encyclopedia*: Tong-Zhi and LGBT Youth in China (co-authored). E-mail: <qrodgef@ yahoo.com>.

Keith Goddard, director of the Gays and Lesbians of Zimbabwe (GALZ), has been active in the LGBT movement in Zimbabwe since 1992. He is also a musician and composer. E-mail: <director@ galz.co.zw>.

Jan M. Goodman has worked in the field of education for thirty years, as a teacher for kindergarten through eighth grade, an elementary school principal, a curriculum writer, a researcher, and a professional development consultant. She currently is the coordinator for Berkeley Unified School District's Beginning Teacher Support and Assessment Program. E-mail: <Jngdmn7@aol.com>.

Pat Griffin is a professor emerita in the Social Justice Education Department at the University of Massachusetts Amherst. Her research and writing interests focus on heterosexism/homophobia and sexism in education, as well as lesbian and gay teachers and students, with a special interest in heterosexism/homophobia in athletics. Dr. Griffin is co-editor of *Teaching for Diversity and Social Justice: A Sourcebook for Teachers and Trainers* (1997). She is the author of *Strong Women, Deep Closets: Homophobia and Lesbians in Sport* (1998). E-mail: <griffin@educ.umass.edu>.

Sarah E. Holmes, MS, is a former Urvashi Vaid Research Fellow at the Policy Institute of the National Gay and Lesbian Task Force.

Madelaine Imber, Australia.

Kevin Jennings is a former high school history teacher and co-founder and executive director of GLSEN (the Gay, Lesbian and Straight Education Network), which brings together teachers, parents, and community members to end anti-LGBT bias in primary and secondary schools. Mr. Jennings is also the author of several books, most recently *Always My Child: A Parent's Guide to Understanding Your Gay, Lesbian, Bisexual, Transgendered or Questioning Son or Daughter.* E-mail: <kjennings@glsen.org>.

Timothy R. Juday holds a PhD in health services research from Johns Hopkins University and a master's degree in public affairs from the University of Texas at Austin. He is an assistant professor in the Department of Public Health Sciences and Epidemiology, University of Hawaii at Manoa, Honolulu, Hawaii, where he teaches health services administration, epidemiology, and evaluation of HIV prevention and care. E-mail: <juday@hawaii.edu>.

Akihiko Komiya is a PhD candidate at Waseda University (Tokyo) and is doing comparative studies on LGBT youth in the United Kingdom and Japan. He is also a part-time teacher of foreign language at a high school. One of his papers is "Description of Homosexual Youth for Prescription for Homophobia" (*Youth Science,* Volume 1). He serves as a member of the editorial board of the Kikan SEXUALITY Eidell Kenkyujo Publishing Co. He is also interested in problematizing heterosexism in foreign language acquisition and ethnocentrism in LGBT studies. E-mail: <komiyaUK@hotmail.com>.

Camille Lee is a doctoral student in social justice education at the University of Massachusetts Amherst where she has been a research assistant for the project Making Schools Safe for LGBT Students. Previous to her current position, Camille was a high school science teacher and gay-straight alliance advisor in Salt Lake City, Utah. E-mail: <cam@educ.umass.edu>.

Lance Trevor McCready earned his PhD and master's degrees in social and cultural studies from the University of California, Berkeley, with a designated emphasis in women and gender studies. His research and writing revolves around various aspects of sexual politics in urban education. He is currently the assistant professor of educational studies at Carleton College, where he teaches classes in multicultural education; gender, sexuality, and schooling; and *Brown vs. Board of Education.* E-mail: <lmccread@carleton.edu>.

Íde O'Carroll is a research associate at the Centre for Gender Studies, Trinity College, Dublin, Ireland. She has researched programs on social exclusion, equality, gender, and migration in Ireland, the European Union, and the United States. She co-edited, with Eoin Collins, *Lesbian and Gay Visions of Ireland: Toward the Twenty-First Century* (Cassells, 1995). E-mail: <ideocarroll@post.harvard.edu>.

Keiko Ofuji is a lecturer at Bates College in the Department of German, Russian, and East Asian Languages and Literatures. E-mail: <kofuji@bates.edu>.

William F. Pinar teaches curriculum theory at Louisiana State University, where he serves as the St. Bernard Parish Alumni Endowed Professor. He has also served as the Frank Talbott Professor at the University of Virginia and the A. Lindsay O'Connor Professor of American Institutions at Colgate University. He taught at the University of Rochester (New York) from 1972 to 1985. He has held visiting appointments at Teachers College, Columbia University, The Ohio State University, the Ontario Institute for Studies in Education, the University of Alberta, and the University of British Columbia, among other institutions. Among Pinar's books are *Autobiography, Politics, and Sexuality* (Peter Lang, 1994) and *The Gender of Racial Politics and Violence in America* (Peter Lang, 2001).

Kathleen Quinlivan is a research associate, Education Department, University of Canterbury, Australia.

Mary Lou Rasmussen is a lecturer, School of Social Cultural Studies in Education, Deakin University, Australia. Currently she is studying Butlerian notions of melancholia in relation to the production of sexualities and genders in educational contexts. In addition, Mary Lou is involved in developing an international collaborative research project utilizing ethnographic work to consider how gender and sexual identities are created in diverse school and community contexts. E-mail: <rasmusml@deakin.edu.au>.

Ronni Sanlo holds a doctorate in education from the University of North Florida. Her area of expertise is sexual and gender identity issues in education and higher education. Ronni is the director of the UCLA Lesbian Gay Bisexual Transgender (LGBT) Campus Resource Center and a lecturer in the UCLA Graduate School of Education. She lives on campus as a faculty in residence. Formerly, Ronni was the LGBT center director at the University of Michigan. She is the originator of the award-winning Lavender Graduation, an event that celebrates the lives and achievements of LGBT students. E-mail: <RSanlo@saonet.ucla.edu>.

Maayan-Rahel Simon is a native Israeli, presently living within the San Francisco Bay Area. She is pursuing her JD with an emphasis on community studies and aspires to work as a lawyer in the social justice fields. Currently her professional life entails working as a caseworker for a court-affiliated, restorative justice–based nonprofit program. She can also be found organizing for social justice causes, specifically on queer/genderqueer and women's issues, and as an antiracist and labor activist. Her passion for organizing lies in her dedication to community and grassroots coalition building. E-mail: <Maayan@thetomatoavenger.org>.

Patti Capel Swartz holds a PhD in English with a specialization in American literature from Claremont Graduate University. She is an assistant professor of English at Kent State University, East Liverpool Campus, Ohio, where she teaches children's and young adult literature, composition, women's literature, and ethnic and other American literatures. E-mail <pswartz@eliv.kent.edu>.

Laura A. Szalacha holds an EdD from Harvard University's Graduate School of Education. She is trained in developmental psychology, with particular foci on adolescent psychosexual development and research methodologies, as well as quantitative, qualitative, and mixed-methods approaches. Her research includes an examination of the dimensions of adolescent lesbian sexual identity, normative development among racial/ethnic minority adolescents and children, resilience and discrimination among sexual and ethnic/racial minorities, and safe schools programs for LGBTQQI students. Having taught at Smith College, Boston University, and Brown University, Laura is currently a researcher at Northeastern University's Center for Work and Learning. E-mail: <l.szalacha@neu.edu.>

Gerald Walton survived grade school and ex-gay ministries to eventually become a doctoral candidate in the Faculty of Education at Queen's University in Kingston, Ontario. His research focus is on bullying as a social and political construct and its implications for improved safe schools policies, especially concerning gay, lesbian, bisexual, and transgender students. His research and advocacy have been featured in interviews for radio, TV, and newspaper; presentations at community meetings and academic conferences; and workshops on homophobia in schoolyard bullying. E-mail: <gwalton@sfu.ca>.

Jeffrey Waugh has completed his graduate studies in the Social Justice Education Program at the University of Massachusetts Amherst. He also holds a master's degree in student affairs and leadership studies from Azusa Pacific University in California, and a bachelor's in business management and communications from Pennsylvania State University. His fourteen-year career in student affairs and higher education includes being a cofounder of California State University, Monterey Bay. Currently he works in private practice and lives in Hatfield, Massachusetts, with his partner David Ellis. E-mail: <jeffrey_a_waugh@hotmail.com>.

Foreword

This book is a milestone for the *Journal of Gay & Lesbian Issues in Education* and for me personally, as one of the journal's associate editors and as a gay teacher. Its contents, chosen by the editor, span topics from the struggles of GLBT teens for self-respect, safety, and wellness in Japan, Oceania, Canada, and the United States, to the efficacy and inclusiveness of gay-straight alliances, to making colleges more responsive to transgender student needs, to GLBT-affirmative elementary teacher education in Appalachia.

Reading these chapters, I flashed back to 1982, when I was one of a group of five gay teachers at Cambridge Rindge & Latin School who met monthly for mutual support over chips and salsa at Chi-Chi's restaurant.

Over a period of months, tension arose within our group. Two of us were impatient with the solely recreational nature of our get-togethers. We wanted to use the opportunity to plan action at the school—to petition the administration for a gay-themed faculty workshop or to start a support group for gay and lesbian students. Our colleagues resisted. They did not consider themselves activists, and I suspect they were leery of the politics that had informed our antiwar and antiracism stances at the school.

Despite this initial division, however, over the next few years most members of the group became advocates for school reform for GLBT students and families. We helped with faculty workshops, lobbied successfully for a gay-straight alliance, and were joined in our cause by a number of straight allies.

The isolation and powerlessness that prompted our first meetings at Chi-Chi's persist for GLBT students and educators in many communities today, but many others have leapt ahead. This progress is manifest in the narratives from around the world presented in this volume. Likewise, opportunities are increasing to document and assess these positive developments. Sarah Holmes's and Sean Cahill's chapter and Laura Szalacha's brief historical portrait of the research in this area are, in fact, prologues to a continuously growing body of work.

Nevertheless—and despite the pervasive Internet—teachers, students, and parents in much of the non-Western world and in many communities within Western nations still struggle to negotiate nonheteronormativity in their schools. They do so in cultural contexts which should remind educators in such places as San Francisco, London, or Paris that the categorical verities and behavioral codes that many of us take for granted have always been situational, relative, and shifting. Readers are cautioned to be wary of Western hegemonic constructions of sexuality. Yet they must be struck in this book, as I have been, by some challenging—and in a sense delightful—encounters between theory and practice. Two examples come immediately to mind.

First, Mary Lou Rasmussen, an Australian lecturer, responds to a biographical piece by Rachel Bromley, one of three "youth voices" in Section I. The theoretically versed Rasmussen recommends that schools help students like Rachel Bromley understand the "irony of identity"—that by deconstructing such essentialist categories as "lesbian," young people will come to appreciate their power to construct their own unique sexualities. Bromley, a New Zealand lesbian and college graduate, responds, "Many students have already come to the realization that they are gay. They may find that someone telling them that they can construct an identity patronizing, which in turn creates an even bigger problem of self-doubt." For this student, a deconstructionist approach that is supposed to yield a greater sense of autonomy instead feels like a setback. The dialogue necessarily ends. Yet what an opportunity for the reader to imagine Rasmussen and Bromley having another go at persuasion or synthesis!

A second instance of the unexpected occurs when Akihiko Komiya reacts to the commentary on his observations on being gay in Japan. The reader has already been informed by the editor that Western homophobia has essentially spoiled the Edenlike homosexual possibilities of ancient Japan. But Akihiko unexpectedly admonishes, "We also have to beware of Orientalism in the field of education and gay studies around the globe."

Such provocative moments, as well as its informative chapters on exemplary programs and practices, make this book a great read. *Gay, Lesbian, and Transgender Issues in Education* provides both a compelling international panorama and a thoughtful analysis of the status of sexual minority students today.

Arthur Lipkin, EdD
Independent scholar

Preface

When the first issue of the *Journal of Gay & Lesbian Issues in Education* appeared in the fall of 2003, it evidenced the natural evolution of scholarship, practice, and policy analysis on queer youth and education. Although research on youth (at least gay or lesbian college students) had been going steadily on since the 1970s, it was not until the late 1980s that educators, researchers, and major educational associations began to address this topic in earnest. During this past generation there has been enormous progress in developing educational policies, practices, and programs as well as conducting scholarship and research. However, as in many other fields, practitioners, policymakers, and scholars—and their clients—have inhabited different worlds, spoken in unrelated tongues, and read dissimilar journals or magazines. The *Journal of Gay & Lesbian Issues in Education* has sought to bridge these divides as well as show commitment to multicultural and international coverage.

Disseminating ideas to an intellectually minded community while drawing implications to educational policy and practice, the inaugural volume included an array of articles, essays, and special features. From queer youth in South Africa and China to Japan and New Zealand, from a British Columbian resource program for educators to an Australian teachers' guidebook, from U.S.-based gay-straight alliances to globalization of queer identities, from psychoanalytic analyses of Canadian physical education (PE) teachers to a program preparing Appalachian teachers, from college policies on transgender youth to teaching about sexuality in relation to media studies, from LBGTQ (lesbian, bisexual, gay, transgender, queer) funding strategies to annotated research, policy analyses, and book reviews, this collective effort among persons across six continents has brought together a variety of voices and discourses for improving the quality of education worldwide.

Gay, Lesbian, and Transgender Issues in Education is the editor's selection from this first volume. The intent is to present a sampling of these articles and essays that—as a group—provide a timely primer for parents and resource for educators as well as those training to enter into schools. Here bullying, transgender students, gay-straight alliances, race and racism, and HIV education are detailed. *Gay, Lesbian, and Transgender Issues in Education* also grounds research-based articles and descriptions of programs and policies with the voices of queer youth. In so doing, it reminds us what is most important: educating a new generation of youth (regardless of sexual or gender identities) who are as empathetic for "the other" as they are resilient and as tenacious for seeking social justice as they are courageous in being.

SECTION I:
YOUTH VOICES

Reflections on Growing Up
Lesbian in New Zealand, Australia,
and the United States

The *Journal of Gay & Lesbian Issues in Education* is different from most academic journals that focus on youth in its incorporation of an international youth advisory board (YAB) whose purpose is to include youth voices and to provide feedback and commentary regarding its content. The YAB is still growing and invites interested youth ages sixteen to twenty-four, particularly outside North America, to join us in making an important and continued presence in the journal. Contact assistant editor Brent E. Cagle at <brentc@bellsouth.net>.

Following are three brief essays written by young women who share personal experiences within their respective educational systems. Contributing editors reflect on the essays, and the essayists have the final word.

Chapter 1

My Story

Rachel Bromley

My story of being a lesbian in New Zealand in the twenty-first century is not that strange, unusual, or even different from many young women who come out as lesbians in their late teens. My story is one of determination, disgust with societal values, difficulties with parents, and concern regarding losing friends and family. I guess, most important, this is a story of me being true to myself and to those I really care about.

From a very early age, I was determined to understand and to try and change the way the world treated boys differently than girls. I come from a family of four girls, so I never had to fight for special treatment with regard to a brother or anything. But I soon realized that I would have to prove myself within the conformist small city in which we lived.

The little things that people "believed in" or made important really annoyed me. For example, on Friday afternoons, my school had sports afternoons. Boys were given an option of playing either rugby or soccer; girls, on the other hand, had one and only one option: netball.

I despised netball because it was boring, there was no physical contact, and there was no real competition. As girls, we were often told, "We are not out here to win. We are here to have fun." This didn't interest me, so I innocently asked my teacher: "Why can't I play rugby or soccer? I don't like netball." I was given a surprised look and told, "Girls don't play 'boy' sports; they enjoy girl sports like netball." "But why?" I asked. She looked me in the eyes and shouted, "Don't backchat me, Rachel! Girls and boys are different. They don't play the same sports or do the same things." Now, I want to make it clear: this particular event didn't have a massive impact on me in regards to me being a lesbian. But right then and there, I knew the world was not a kind place and did not really accept difference or even consider its possibilities.

Time went on, and I began high school. My friends would talk about boys and who they thought was hot, and they would ask me whom I thought was a hottie. I would tell them straightforwardly that I thought the boys had no prospects and were losers. Their reaction was not really surprising; they just called me a feminist, which made me smile.

At the age of fifteen, I knew I was a lesbian, and this frightened me beyond belief. My parents were devout Christians. I was told when very young that only men marry women, and they don't have sex until marriage. As part of the church, my sisters and I attended camp every summer. The ideology of the camp itself was credible, but the rules that were enforced were odd—to say the least. Girls and boys were not allowed to sit together or to socialize. Only men spoke at the two three-hour lectures each day, which disturbed me, since I didn't think this was right. This enforcement of so-called Christian doctrine made me afraid of coming out not only to myself but also to my parents.

After that summer, I didn't go to Christian camps; I became depressed and angry at being gay. All I wanted was to be "normal" and to make my parents happy. I quickly learned that making my parents happy was easy if only I would lie to myself for the rest of my life. I wasn't prepared to do this, nor did I have a desire to live the life of my parents.

In the year 2000, I went to University of Canterbury to achieve academically and to come out in a place that had approximately six times as many people as my home city. I was also innocent and, if I'm honest about it, I was ignorant. For years, I dreamed about coming out in a larger city and believed that the imagined gay community would be friendly and supportive—and even that in the wider society being lesbian or gay would *not* be an issue. I quickly found this to be false.

At the university's residence hall, I was constantly reminded that heterosexuality was the be-all and end-all of life. One time, the halls had a "secret admirer week," and girls were given guys' room numbers to leave "presents." There was no option for girls to be other girls' admirers (or guys and guys, for that matter).

So even in this larger place, coming out was difficult. I wasn't ready emotionally. I needed to think things through and plan my coming out to friends and family. A year passed by before I went to the on-campus gay and lesbian support group. It was great to see other people who were gay and lesbian. But my battle was not so much in finding other gay people as it was in coming out to my parents and other family members. Here, I had support from some straight friends who were just wonderful.

At the age of nineteen, I called my parents from my flat. I told them after some discussion about differences and acceptance. My mum said, "What are you saying? Are you a lesbian?" I answered, "Yes." Mum cried. She told me all of the "fun" consequences I would be faced with (like going to hell). My dad didn't talk about it.

I knew my parents and their beliefs, but it still didn't stop the hurt I felt. I'm not going to lie; it was difficult to know that I had broken my parents' hearts and all their hopes and dreams.

For almost a year and a half, it felt as if I had no parents and no support. I guess what really kept me going was that I knew I was a strong person and that I wanted to make a change in the world.

I hope to begin a master's of social work degree in the near future. I want to work with young people who are coming out and tell them, "Yes, it's really hard, but it gets better. You just have to be strong and believe there is something really fantastic just down the road."

I want to make a difference for young queer people. I want them to believe that being queer is special and not to hate themselves for feeling "different" from "normal society." I want change, and I know I can achieve that at some point! I have built up lots of fabulous and wonderful networks of support and friendships since I came out. You just have to believe something fantastic is out there and strive to achieve it. In the end, you have to be true to yourself, because that's what really matters!

Chapter 2

What I Would Have Liked
My Teachers to Know

Madelaine Imber

What I would have liked my teachers to know is that I'm no different. I know that doesn't give teachers a fair guide, so I'll elaborate, but first a little history.

Growing up in Australia, I went to a relatively conservative private school in the inner city. As a uniting church school, it was also relatively liberal in its teachings. A lot of my teachers were also my friends. I was the model student: editor of the student newspaper, captain of the first girls' cricket team, in the debating team, in the choir, the full complement. I spent lunchtimes evenly divided between my few friends and the English office.

But beyond that—in fact during it all—my marks dropped; I lost confidence and self-esteem. I realized I liked girls, and that was not okay. It was what queer jokes were made of. Lesbianism was not real; it didn't exist, not in this cushy middle-class world.

The thing that I most remember, what sticks in my mind of that time, is Year 11 English. Our teacher, let us call her Ms. H, wanted us to practice for our final year creative writing folio. She gave us the topic "A Different Type of Friend." I was a little stuck. The only thing I could think of was *my* friend, who I had a major crush on. But she was a girl.

Stuff it! I thought. *That's a different type of friend.* I mean, that's the type of different type of friend *I wish* I had. And they always say, write about what you know. I did. I wrote about what was in my heart and what I couldn't tell anyone. I thought I could trust Ms. H; maybe it was time to test the waters to see how people would react.

For a week I absolutely panicked. Every English class, I feared the counselor would come in and I'd be carted out. Ms. H finally handed back the piece—without a mark and with a "please see me" attached. I panicked. The next day (after a sleepless night), she hauled me up to her desk to speak about it. I almost threw up.

The class was working on something else, but the first row could hear everything. My deepest, darkest secret was in this woman's hands. She looked at my work again, told me there was something wrong with the structure or the last paragraph didn't make sense; I don't even remember. I agreed with everything, terrified she'd mention the content, expose me as I really was but couldn't admit to being. Deep down, I wanted her to say something—not there or then but maybe in my frequent trips to the staff room—but she never did.

Looking back on it, it was one of the first disclosures of who I am. I still have the essay. The structure was crap. But it represents much more than that.

What does my story say about how to work with young people? In this case, speak to the student or at least be open and available. Do not *ever* avoid the issue.

Overall, I had relatively good experiences with the staff. My cricket coach was my buddy. *But* when the girls on my team flinched as I approached them or when they would not talk to me, he was blissfully ignorant. When I could clear a locker room by walking into it, when the dyke jokes were sniggered at, followed by an awkward silence, the staff did not see or chose to ignore what was going on. Teachers are not oblivious to student harassment and the politics of various friendship groups. I'm uncertain whether these teachers really didn't notice or they just didn't know what to do.

I didn't want special treatment. I wanted to be normal; I wanted my sexuality to be treated as part of the diversity of the school environment, not ignored. The staff was always really supportive of my writing and so on. But in class and in all discussions, love was heterosexual; marriage was the ideal. Sex was not taboo necessarily, but it was specifically straight. Gays were drag queens and lesbians were nonexistent. Youth suicide was a problem, pregnancy was an issue, condoms were vital (but what's a dental dam?), sex was safe, AIDS (acquired immunodeficiency syndrome) and STDs (sexually transmitted diseases) were a worry, straight love and romance were beautiful. They weren't squeamish about sex at my school—just about sexuality.

What could my teachers have done? I really wish they had just been there. Not asking me about my boyfriend. Not asking who I was going to the formal with, and then asking if he's my boyfriend. (Actually, his boyfriend went with my girlfriend, and whose hand do you think was on my thigh that evening?) Not saying, with a raised eyebrow, "I saw you at St Kilda beach!" when I know they saw me at the beach—kissing my girlfriend. What did I want them to do? Not ignore it. Not treat me like I was some sort of special case, but not ignore that everyone is special. All I really wanted was to be looked in the eye and told: "You're okay." 'Cause I am.

Today, I'm finished with school, with uni, and am now in the workforce. I have worked in schools for the past six years altogether, running workshops about homosexuality and homophobia. Some days in the paper, I see stories about law reform or young GLBTI groups in the suburbs. I meet young men who are happy to find a doctor who is gay. Other days, I see lesbian mothers who are struggling to claim legal rights to take care of their children; transgender youths who are contemplating suicide; and young teachers who are bullying lesbian students.

A huge silence still exists around sexual diversity education. The school has a huge impact on the response we get from students when discussing sexuality and homophobia. An open and accepting environment allows students to work through homophobia, break down any stereotypes or issues they have, and think critically about the issues confronting them and their classmates. However, a large number of schools don't allow these issues to be discussed and instead try to silence those students brave enough to speak out. The teachers in these schools (no matter how progressive they are) are scared to address GLBTI issues. They fear losing their jobs, being outed, or parent complaints. This leads to a conspiracy of silence in which teachers and students feel that they can't speak out. This is damaging not only for GLBTI youth but also for society; narrow-minded and bigoted students and teachers make for a restrictive and backward community.

In schools, these issues need to be addressed across the board, not just in a "sex ed" environment. I still see GLBTI issues focused so much around sexual behavior, AIDS, and sex-reassignment surgery, instead of around diverse lifestyles and alternative notions of family and society. From a young age, students should be exposed to different types of families. Not everyone had a mum and a dad; some families have two mums or two dads (or both!).

I hope that when my kids are asked to write about a different kind of friend, lesbianism isn't so different—that it's just a part of the full trajectory of relationships in which young people engage.

Chapter 3

On Being "Queer"

Maayan-Rahel Simon

My coming out as queer wasn't an act of acceptance as much as it was a rejection of every message that confined me to a role of pleasing other people by denying myself. From early experiences in elementary school to the time that I came out my last year of middle school, I was tortured by the constant struggle of following the unspoken rules of how I was supposed to act and react as a heterosexual woman in American society. I wanted more than anything to relate to the world outside of me. Instead, I was forced to play witness to a world in which I clearly did not belong.

In school, binary gender and sexuality were enforced without question. It was made clear to my female classmates and me that, as young women, our power and authority were lodged in how males regarded us. I watched the independence of every girl around me shrivel up and shrink each time a boy, aggressively waving his hand in the air and falling lopsided out of his desk, was called on and praised for his intelligence while, as girls, we were considered unmannerly for expressing our voices. While our male classmates were expected to develop a strong sense of themselves and excel academically, we were encouraged to see ourselves as "smart" if we were popular, pleasant, and sociable. Nearly all of my female classmates went from being vivacious and confident to regarding themselves primarily in terms of their outward appearance and how attractive men found them to be.

Because of this inequality, I grew to resent my gender as an obstacle and a symbol of oppression. I was saturated in the socially constructed messages, which defined being a woman as being confined to the wishes of a husband and not playing an important role in the world. When women were acknowledged in the community or the media, their gender was often so overtly hyped that it undermined why they were being honored in the first place. Surrounded by Barbie and Ken dolls and big-breasted British pop singers sporting clunky high heels and short shorts, I was stranded without strong female role models that validated and supported my strength as a creative, free-thinking individual. Instead, I was ostracized and teased—and then blamed by my teachers for not working harder to "get along."

Discovering my sexuality became a celebration of enjoying my body and independence as *mine,* not just as part of another person's experience. "Queer" became my mantra for breaking away from accepting my role as it was given to me and reclaiming myself as a whole person. It was my refusal to be compartmentalized into the clothes I wear, the way I speak, the body I'm in, the holidays I celebrate, the people I choose to be with. My place as a lesbian woman became a wonderful ritual, not a burden. Suddenly, I found righteous female and transgender role models everywhere; I began working to follow in their steps by using my experiences to act as a witness for other negatively targeted communities. Rather than being envious or resentful of men because I could not have the same privileges, I found that my dedication to myself as a queer woman freed me to appreciate all genders and sexualities for their uniqueness.

Although *queer* is a word that carries a sad weight and a history of devastating violence, I find that it is the truest reflection of how I feel within a predominantly homophobic and heterosexist culture. I choose to identify as queer because where *lesbian* suggests only that my orientation is sexually related, *queer* associates me with a movement to reclaim myself and come out from under my oppression. By using my daily experiences of being alienated and discriminated against, I am better able to act as an ally for others and truly hear the stories of marginalized, exploited, and underrepresented people.

To embrace the term *queer* within "gay and lesbian culture" is to finally put an accurate name to all of the feelings of awkwardness and insecurity in being uncomfortable with our desires and affections as nonheterosexual individuals in a heterosexist society. We are taking back who we are and proclaiming that we will not tolerate being made to feel abnormal or told that we are mentally ill. We are refusing to accept gender and sexuality as ideas that are imposed on us. Instead, they should be seen as a reflection and celebration of who we are as a community of individuals who are both sexual, sensual people and strong, passionate, and creative contributors to the world.

Chapter 4

Commentaries

Here, several distinguished educators with various backgrounds and from different countries were asked to comment following their reading of these essays. Given space limitations, these are more evocative than particulate, but collectively they provide multiple platforms for reflection. Similarly brief concluding remarks from Madelaine, Maayan-Rahel, and Rachel follow these commentaries.

In a recent article, Claire Colebrook (2000) ponders the irony of identity. She observes something of an identity paradox, a situation in which we are all marked by "the impossibility of *self*-definition as well as the unavoidability of the self as *position*" (p. 27). I want to use this quote as a point of departure to discuss these three young women's reflections on growing up lesbian in Australia, New Zealand, and the United States.

A common theme is the struggle to define themselves and to find acceptance from family, peers, and teachers. These young women wished they had met with more acceptance and recognition of their sexual and gendered selves throughout the compulsory years of schooling and beyond. Together, these recollections alert me to the discrimination that young people experience when they don't conform to normative notions of gender and sexuality.

Reading between the lines, I was also struck by the strength that permeated these reflections. Each woman is an articulate, strong, and critical thinker with a genuine desire to forge a better path for the next generation of students who identify as lesbian, gay, bisexual, transgender, or intersex (LGBTI).

How might teachers and teacher educators join with such young women in approaching their conundrum: acknowledge their desire for acceptance yet reject the notion that LGBTI students are all alike and/or all have the same needs? How can educators acknowledge the diverse sexualities and genders that enliven school cultures without carving out LGBTI students as always and already different from their peers, reinscribing a binary that often does more harm than good?

Rachel Bromley suggests that a way of fostering young people who identify as LGBTI might be to allow them the space to be true to themselves, while Madelaine Imber envisages an environment where "lesbianism isn't so different—that it's just a part of the full trajectory of relationships in which young people engage." Following Imber and Bromley's suggestions, I want to argue for a sexuality education in schools that requires students and teachers to *reflect* on how people come to recognize themselves as being gay *or* straight *or* trans *or* bisexual.

One way in which sexuality education might enact this strategy is by acknowledging that sexual and gender identities are not essential and, therefore, predestined. By acknowledging that lesbians are not all "born that way" but rather have some capacity to construct their own identities, teachers are inviting young people to reflect on the construction of their own identities. Such an opening up of conversation might allow a student who thinks she cannot possibly *be* transgender or lesbian to consider how these identities influence her own sense of self, regardless of how she chooses to identify.

I advocate this approach for two reasons. First, this strategy doesn't call on teachers and students to single-handedly solve the problems associated with homophobia and heterosexism that emerge in these young women's narratives (surely asking teachers or students to embark on such a task only sets them up to fail, as such problems are influenced by powerful discourses that circulate beyond the school). Second, such an approach moves the focus away from a preoccupation with how individuals are controlled by others, which is not to say that we should ignore such constraints, but it is to recognize that young people's ability to stamp out homophobia is necessarily limited.

For me, reflecting on how I continue to become lesbian, *or* straight, *or* queer (all of which I have been at one time or another) is part of a process of being "true" to myself. This process isn't so much a search for who I "really" am (as this continues to change at a rapid rate and I don't think that I ever want to pin myself down). Instead, it is an acknowledgement that I am constantly becoming something and that I want to be thoughtful about this ongoing process of becoming.

Focusing on the relationship of the self to the self, to paraphrase Michel Foucault (1996), helps me to think differently about the way I can care for my self—and for others. So for me, being true to myself isn't so much about coming out; rather, it's about continually negotiating the irony of identity (to borrow from Colebrook, 2000). It's about recognizing that sexualities and genders, in all their diverse forms, are constantly in a state of negotiation and flux.

Ladelle McWhorter (1999) argues that this understanding of the relationship of the self to the self helps her to act despite (and even because of) her experience of discrimination as somebody who identifies as a lesbian. Similarly, Maayan-Rahel Simon envisages people who have the capacity to act and identify as sexual, sensual, strong, passionate, and creative. In short, I am arguing that an appreciation of the irony of identity may help young people—and adults—foster practices in their lives which enable themselves and others to fulfill Simon's vision.

Mary Lou Rasmussen
Lecturer
School of Social Cultural Studies in Education
Deakin University

Perhaps it's the mother in me, or the lesbian child who desperately dreaded coming out all those years ago, or the educator and activist, or perhaps pieces of each that make me want to hold these young writers and tell them that their courage, their passion, and their self-love fill my heart—and bring tears to my eyes. Their words also remind me of questions that I've pondered for years: Why does Rachel in New Zealand describe a similar story and the same emotional phenomenon as Maayan-Rahel in the United States and Madelaine in Australia? Continents away, why are their stories eerily parallel? Generations away, why do at least pieces of their stories so vividly match my own?

While each story poignantly shares Rachel's, Maayan-Rahel's, and Madelaine's experiences of fear and denial and rejection, a common thread of resilience lies deep within the hearts of all three. Each of these women knows who she is. Each has no doubt about her sexual and gender identities. Their resilience, their desire to survive, is palpable. Their courage and self-love in the face of oppression is beautifully charged and passionately shared. While each experienced what Lucozzi (1998) described as intolerant environments, each understood her internal capacity and desire to rebound in the face of adversity (Ryan, 2001). Perhaps it is this phenomenon of resilience that ties together the experiences of the three young women despite the fact that they are continents apart.

Queer and *faggot* were the only words I heard to describe homosexuality as a high school student in the early 1960s. The subject was patently taboo. I tried so hard to find a reflection of my young lesbian self somewhere, anywhere, hoping to find evidence that I wasn't the only one. All I found was a definition of homosexuality in the 1962 *Encyclopedia Britannica* that described men who had sex with other men in a sadistic, mentally ill sort of way. As a girl who loved other girls, I had no reflection of my existence.

Queer and *faggot* were common taunts back in the 1960s—just as they often are today. If one wore green to school on Thursdays, then one was surely queer and everyone mercilessly harassed the person. I avoided green on Thursdays. High school was a terribly painful time and place for me. Unlike Rachel, Maayan-Rahel, and Madelaine, who refused to accept the status quo, I lived a parallel life: Straight Ronni was an excellent student, an outstanding musician, a decent surfer, and the president of a school social club. She worked excruciatingly hard to fit it so that no one would notice the parallel Queer Ronni. I referred to myself in the third person as That Damned Queer each time I looked into the mirror, and I lived in constant fear of discovery, trusting neither family nor friends. I was in love with girls. Boys held no interest or mystique for me, forcing me to lie to friends, family, and myself. I had sex with boys because I thought it would make this queer thing go away. In my fear of being rejected by everyone in my life, I deliberately remained aloof. Refusing to become close to anyone for fear my secret world would surely be revealed. It's ironic to me that forty years later the big secret of my young life is now the work of my whole life.

Working with lesbian, gay, bisexual, and transgender college students, I marvel at their resilience—the same resilience described by Rachel, Maayan-Rahel, and Madelaine—as their adolescent struggles brought them from high school to college. Their ability to succeed in the face of constant harassment, their strength, and their deep love of self is amazing to me. While their journeys are individually unique, each exemplifies an ability to rise above adversity to a place of honor and integrity and appreciation for their sexual and gender identities. These powerful young women are among those who remind me daily exactly why I do this work.

Ronni Sanlo
Director
UCLA Lesbian Gay Bisexual Transgender
Campus Resource Center

Although these three essays are written by young lesbians from three different countries, the women share a common journey: from social alienation to self-affirmation. They all describe an early awareness that they did not fit in the heterosexual world. In an effort to be "normal," they were forced to deny their sexual orientation to family, friends and, sometimes, themselves. They were strangers in their environments, with no positive intervention from their local school systems. Madelaine, a self-described "model student," recognized that "I liked girls and that was not okay. . . . [It's] not real; it didn't exist, not in this cushy middle-class world." Rachel realized she was a lesbian at age fifteen and "This frightened me beyond belief" because it directly contradicted her parents' Christian beliefs and those of the larger society. Maayan-Rahel states that in elementary and middle school, she was "tortured by the constant struggle of following the unspoken rules of how I was supposed to act and react as a heterosexual woman in American society." Each woman describes a painful conflict between awareness of their sexual orientation and the values of the dominant culture. This isolation estrangement from the norm contributed to intense feelings of inadequacy and low self-esteem.

In all three essays, schools are mentioned as agents of institutionalized oppression. When Madelaine takes a risk to come out to her teacher in a writing assignment, Ms. H only comments on the structure of the essay; the message is ignored. At Madelaine's school, antigay harassment was ignored by staff who often assumed that all girls would have boyfriends. In sixth grade, Rachel was told that girls couldn't play "'boy' sports," and in college, she was "constantly reminded that heterosexuality was the be-all and end-all of life." Maayan-Rahel witnessed acute sexism in school. "It was made clear to my female classmates and me that, as young women, our power and authority were lodged in how males regarded us." The main function of these educational systems was to enforce and perpetuate the heterosexual norm.

Despite unsupportive experiences in schools, these three women moved past alienation to a feeling of self-acceptable, pride, and affirmation. All have become powerful lesbians/queer women who find an inner strength in the fact that they *are* different. Madelaine works in schools to educate people about homosexuality and homophobia. Rachel hopes to become a social worker and "make a difference for young queer people." Maayan-Rahel uses her understanding of oppression to become an ally to "marginalized, exploited, and underrepresented people."

Each of these three essays ends on a positive note. However, all educators have a responsibility to intervene in the cycle of oppression that too often continues to deny the existence and rights of sexual minority youth. We must build powerful alliances and take a stand to advocate for inclusion of sexual orientation issues throughout the curriculum at all grade levels. We must work for policies to end harassment and violence against GLBTQ students or those perceived to be GLBTQ; we must implement programs to address the needs of sexual minority youth. If we carry out our responsibility to make schools safe for all students, regardless of sexual orientation, the journey from alienation to self-affirmation will not be as fraught as it was for these three courageous young women.

Jan M. Goodman
Principal
King Middle School
California

Your narratives reach across continents to me in Lismore, Ireland, telling of growing up lesbian. I caution myself that your accounts are individual examples of lives lived in New Zealand, Australia, and the United States. My response to reading your words is also personal. I can truly only say at this point: Here is a middle-aged Irish woman responding to stories of three young women's experiences. Why do I begin this way, you might well wonder?

I'm interested in social policy and in the way personal experience, researched convincingly, can be shown to reflect a collective experience. I have witnessed the use of personal narratives (in conjunction with other evidence) as a powerful tool to shift the position of government and, ultimately, generate change in relation to equality in society. This has happened in a range of areas, including education. Why is policy important? Positions taken at the government level filter down to school practice—at least in theory, in schools financially supported by the state.

Reading your texts, I realize that the most striking point of commonality across your narratives of educational journeys is the damage of denial. All of you write that it was harmful to be ignored or dismissed as lesbian within the education system you navigated as young women. All speak of a desire to be treated with respect and to be true to your selves. You remind me that the first point of departure toward respect is acknowledgment of difference, or, as you put it so well, Madelaine, "I wanted my sexuality to be treated as part of the diversity of the school environment, not ignored."

However, I have learned that policymakers have to be convinced of the need for change, to be "sold" the value of diversity within state-supported educational communities. Yet some educators with strong religious positions may never be convinced, and I'm struck by the references to church-based education in two of your narratives. Of course, we need to hear and read of lesbian journeys; so few are represented in the public domain in Western societies. But we must also be strategic when truth telling. To bring about change, a wide range of approaches needs to be used, including relating stories of personal experience such as you have done here in this journal, reaching educators worldwide.

Let me elaborate. In Ireland, it is said that two women got together for a conversation about their children. One was the conservative Fianna Fáil Party Minister for Justice, Máire Geoghan-Quinn, the other Phil Moore, the mother of a gay boy. The result, some contend, was the decriminalization of homosexuality in Ireland in 1993. I'd like to think that story alone could wield such power, but in fact, the women's meeting was only a small but important strategy in a sophisticated campaign devised and executed by the members of GLEN

(Gay and Lesbian Equality Network, formed in the late 1980s to lobby for law reform and to seek the introduction and implementation of comprehensive legislation to ensure the equal rights of lesbians and gays in Ireland).

There is a valuable lesson to be learned here for those who wish to see change in what may well be the final frontier in the battle for equality, the education system. The challenge must be met on all fronts, with multiple narratives of educational journeys part of the strategy. I find it extremely heartening that all of you have carved out an initial adult life plan designed to correct the harmful and negative experiences of other lesbian and gay youth. You have vowed to be living proof of existence, openly lesbian in primarily heterosexual cultures and societies. Your narratives remind me that in the context of current debates where a great deal of time is spent thinking of harassment and physical violence against lesbians and gays within schools, educators must also think about the covert damage done by silencing your voices in schools.

This leads me back to policy. Why? In addition to policy speaking to issues of harassment and physical harm, it must also address issues of denial by educators who, because of their own unease or prejudice, ignore sexual orientation.

In 1999, I walked into Arlington High School in Massachusetts. There to the right of the principal's office, directly inside the front door, was a huge notice board area completely covered with information and photographs relating to activities of the school's gay-straight alliance. It did my heart good to see such acknowledgment, which you would not find in an Irish school—not yet anyway. In a similar way, it did my heart good to read your pieces.

Íde O'Carroll
Research Associate
Centre for Gender Studies, Trinity College
Dublin, Ireland

REFERENCES

Colebrook, C. (2000). The meaning of irony, *Textual Practice*, 14(1), 5-30.
Foucault, M. (1996). Ethics of concern for the self as a practice of freedom. In S. Lotringer (Ed.), *Foucault live (Interviews, 1961-1984)* (pp. 432-449). New York: Semiotext(E).

Lucozzi, E. (1998). A far better place: Institutions as allies. In R. Sanlo (Ed.), *Working with lesbian, gay, bisexual, and transgender college students: A handbook for faculty and administrators* (pp. 47-52). Westport: CT: Greenwood Press.

McWhorter, L. (1999). *Bodies and pleasures: Foucault and the politics of sexual normalization*. Bloomington: Indiana University Press.

Ryan, C. (2001). Counseling lesbian, gay, and bisexual youths. In A. D'Augelli and C. Patterson (Eds.), *Lesbian, gay, and bisexual identities and youth: Psychological perspectives* (pp. 224-250). New York: Oxford University Press.

Chapter 5

Authors' Reactions

The strong theme that I saw in these responses, especially in Sanlo's commentary, was one of resilience. In my mind, resilience links back to values and self-worth. Young GLBTI youth go through hell—and some don't make it. But there are many who do, who fight tooth and nail just to be themselves.

While no one knows *why* people are GLBTI, it is real—as it has been through history. And even in darker times than these, people have been openly lesbian, gay, bi, or trans. Why do so many people go through this, get knocked down a thousand times, and still get up again? It's an undying belief in themselves. Even when others attempt to beat their difference out of them—be it friends, family, society—there is still a tiny flame of self-worth and the belief that for them there is no other way to be.

If this truth could be translated, harnessed, and used throughout people's lives, imagine the strong leaders with dedication, conviction, and integrity we could have.

I related strongly to Bromley's theme of "being true" to herself, and to Simon's reclaiming of herself as "a whole person." These themes are universal. They come from the path that Sanlo's talks of, the one of self-loathing and "the damned queer" she saw in the mirror. They come from "damage of denial" that O'Carroll writes about, and from Rasmussen's sense of the "damaging binaries" that plague both sexuality and gender. These demons have been conquered by all of us in some capacity—as is witnessed by this written work.

How does this relate to education? All students—be they straight, gay, trans, intersex, in between, or queer—need to be encouraged to listen to that inner voice of resilience and truth. We need to have our integrity nurtured and our convictions heard.

Madelaine Imber

In these writings I read the plea—from both students and adult mentors alike—for educators to take the risk to approach sexuality as real, normal, and human across all spectrums of race, religion, gender, culture, age, and economic background. Beyond continents, generations, academic disciplines, and religious institutions, teachers (as influential figures in young people's lives) can empower and support queer students. Sadly, they can also reinforce the social construction that oppresses so many of us. The real devastation, as Ronni Sanlo makes clear, is that we are beginning to bandage the institutionalized systems of oppression rather than change the systems themselves.

From the choices of reading materials that the teachers are given, to the examples in second-year algebra word problems, it is a rare exception when curriculum isn't heterosexist. "In all three essays, schools are mentioned as agents of institutionalized oppression," writes Jan Goodman. "The main function of these educational systems was to enforce and perpetuate the heterosexual norm."

Many teachers who may otherwise consider themselves to be "open and accepting" in regard to "alternative lifestyles" fail to acknowledge gender aside from "male" and "female" as biological functions. For example, Rachel Bromley shares that she was "constantly reminded that heterosexuality was the be-all and end-all of life" in her daily interactions at her university. Teachers may openly validate being gay or lesbian or queer as natural and normal but then use language that reinforces heterosexuality as the norm and homosexuality as the exception. From elementary school through high school, I experienced this feeling of being separated out or invisible every day: from hearing "when you have a *boyfriend . . .* " from my fourth-grade teacher, to middle school where my math instructor would joke "stop flirting with the boys!" every time a woman didn't understand the curriculum, to third-period high school English in which the entire unit that we spent on pivotal literature of the 1960s and 1970s completely failed to recognize any queer figures.

When my peers and I questioned where queer history fit in, the only feedback that we received was that it was not relevant. *Not relevant?* How could it be any more relevant when in spite of every zero-tolerance policy or piece of state antidiscrimination legislation, the two most-used slurs on my high school campus (not to mention nationwide) are "Faggot!" and "That's so gay/you're gay/stop being gay!" As Íde O'Carroll says, "In the context of current debates where a great deal of time is spent thinking of harassment and physical violence against lesbians and gays within schools, educators must also think about the covert damage done by silencing [their] voices." When queer students are only addressed in terms of mental and physical health and safety, it further reinforces that being queer is something negative, something inflicted upon us that we must survive, not enjoy.

Why can we talk about sperm and eggs and meiosis for an entire semester in biology class, yet the opportunity to talk about the function of sexual organs purely for pleasure, such as masturbation or using our bodies to be intimate with our partners, is virtually nonexistent? I was a fortunate exception to have one lesbian teacher in middle school, and, even so, she was forced to "be discreet," which limited our discussions of sexuality to those of how to best survive in an oppressive environment. Like Madelaine Imber, at my school, "Sex was not taboo necessarily, but it was specifically straight. Gays were drag queens and lesbians were nonexistent." Similarly, my experience in the education system, from first grade to the time that I graduated, was also one in which "they weren't squeamish about sex . . . just about sexuality." Even continents away, I experienced the same lack of validation that my sexual exploration was positive and exciting.

We need to deconstruct sex education and reconstruct a focus on *sexual* education that is not limited to a single discipline and covers all aspects of sexuality. Educators must approach sexuality as a function of sensuality and help students appreciate what it means to identify as heterosexual or homosexual, or anywhere in between. As Mary Lou Rasmussen suggests, if teachers approach the topic of homosexuality by provoking all students to consider their own sexual identities, queer students will be validated without being separated out as different. Similarly, I believe that educators have the power to play a primary role in bringing sexuality into a more realistic light, across every range of gender and sexuality. By exposing all students to the unique culture of the queer community, teachers give queer students the opportunity to acknowledge and discover their sexuality while reinforcing to *everyone* that it is something natural, normal, empowering, and positive.

Maayan-Rahel Simon

"By acknowledging that lesbians are not all 'born that way' but rather have some capacity to construct their own identities," Mary Lou Rasmussen writes, "teachers are inviting young people to reflect on the construction of their own identities." I think this is troubling for several reasons.

Firstly, many people strive to suggest that being gay should not be highlighted in an individual's life. But in reality, this is extremely important to identity formation and issues of conformity versus individuality. To identify as "queer" in a school is to fight against societal norms of the heterosexual world. Second, being told by teachers that some people have the capacity to construct their own identities may help *some* students. I find this problematic. Many students have already come to the realization that they are gay. They may find that someone telling them that they can construct an identity patronizing, which in turn creates an even bigger problem of self-doubt.

Rachel Bromley

Reflections on Being Gay in Japan and China

Chapter 6

Difficulties Japanese Gay Youth Encounter

Akihiko Komiya
Keiko Ofuji (Translator)

Letters

Hokkaido, First Year High School, March 2000

I changed my thoughts about gay men recently when I met a gay man through *Fabulous,* a magazine for gay men. Until then, I didn't like myself because of my being gay. It did not seem "cool" that a man falls in love with a man; it seemed shameful to me. I wrote about such feelings to the person. He wrote back to me, "It is natural that a man falls in love with a man and it is wonderful. You should not feel guilty about your being gay or blame yourself." When I read his letter, I felt so relieved. All of his words made sense to me and made me feel at ease. It was the first time for me to have that kind of feelings because of another person's words. I like myself much more than before.

Aichi Prefecture, Second Year High School, January 2000

Do you honestly live your life without telling a lie? I was not honest until recently. Although I liked men, I said I liked women in front of my friends. Even when I fell in love with a man, I denied my feelings. The more I hid my feelings, the more I felt that I was ugly and was ashamed of myself. I thought those kinds of skills were natural and necessary for a gay man to live in this society. However, a gay friend I met recently lived honestly. He didn't hide his sexuality from his parents, brothers, sisters, friends, or, of course, himself. I felt how uncourageous and timid I was in contrast to him. After I knew him, I was able to change myself. I grew up as a person and as a gay man. I had originally been a cheerful person and nowadays I've become more cheerful. I would like to thank him one day.

Kagoshima Prefecture, Sixteen Years Old, June 2000

I have a problem now. It is about a friendship with my male friends. All of my friends have a girlfriend, so they always ask me, "Why don't you have a girlfriend?" I answer, "Because it is troublesome." My friends introduce me to girls, but it puts me in a dilemma.

I fell in love with a man with a butch haircut who looked shy and handsome, although I was too shy to talk to him. I was thinking about him for two and a half years, imagining some nice things. But recently, I learned that he had a girlfriend and I was shocked. Being a gay among heterosexual male friends is tough. I'm tired of being among them during their discussions of girls, knowing I've lost my love. I feel empty and lonely. I really need a gay friend. . . .

Kanagawa Prefecture, Third Year High School, February 2000

I told my special feeling to my friend who was in the same class and the same club when I was in the second year here in the high school. We did many things together and were good friends. I could not help telling my feelings, although I hesitated a little. Since then, he has completely ignored me. One day, there was a chance to talk to him, so I asked him to tell me why he had been ignoring me. He answered, "I thought you were a good friend, but I was betrayed. I felt disgusted when you told me you loved me." He continued that he was not able to be my friend as before and we should stay away from each other for a while. After that, I have not talked with him at all. We have some other friends in common who are worried about our "quarrel." I would like to fix our broken relationship; however, I am sick and tired of this matter because it has been nearly one year. Sometimes I even feel I don't want to go to school. I have been thinking about my problem so much that my grades have gone down. I'm going to take an entrance exam soon. I am basically an optimistic person, but I am now depressed.

Nineteen Years Old, October 2000

One reason why I'm working a part-time job is that in high school the teachers didn't tell me to live as a gay man. I wanted to get job information related to gay men and wanted to have gay magazines, but I had no idea how I could find them because my home was in a rural area. I couldn't even imagine how I would live my own life as a gay man, which led me not to go to a university or get a certain job. I started working as a part-timer. One day a year ago, I accidentally found *Buddy,* a gay magazine. It was the first time that I read a gay magazine. Then my life changed to what I wanted. I am really relieved and happy now as a gay man. . . .

Saitama Prefecture, Sixteen Years Old, September 2000

I was in trouble because I could not accept that I was a gay man when I was in junior high school. I kept questioning myself, "Why do I fall in love with men?" and thought about committing suicide. Then, I wrote a letter to a column for junior and senior high school students in *Buddy,* a gay magazine. When I received many encouraging letters from all over the country, I changed my thoughts. I accepted the fact that I'm gay and decided to enjoy my life as a gay man.

In this letter, I would like to encourage and empower you who may be in trouble about your sexuality. Many of you, perhaps, don't like yourselves because you are different from your friends in terms of falling in love. Also, you may be worried about your uncertain future and about your family, whether they accept you as you are or not. It is a fact that gay men are still misunderstood in this society, but also it is a fact that there are people who understand and accept us as gay men. People's impression of gay men varies. If you meet a person who accepts you as a gay man, you will be able to lead your life. If you have good and sincere friends, your life will change. I want to have gay friends who went through similar problems and troubles in this homophobic society. Gay friends are precious. You don't have to hide your feelings, unlike when you talk with your schoolmates. You will be able to enjoy your life with your gay friends. Moreover, you will be stronger when you get someone who understands and supports you. Then you won't feel lonely. I want to be the one who understands and supports you.

Finally, please don't commit suicide because of your homosexuality. Being gay is not at all wrong. If you are alive, I will guarantee that you'll have good luck someday!

Reflections on These Letters

I would like to summarize the points of the six letters. The fifth author (the nineteen-year-old) listed two reasons why he works as a part-timer. One is that in his high school, the teachers didn't tell him about gay men. In Japan's schools today, only heterosexuality and heterosexual marriage are taught. No effort is made to show lives of gay men at guidance sessions for students' job hunting. If a student said she or he would like to learn about and have a job concerning handicapped people or women, it would not be a problem. However, it would be extremely hard to say at a guidance session, "I am interested in homosexual issues and would like to learn about their rights and work for them." Moreover, gay students, particularly in rural areas in Japan, don't even know about organizations and systems for learning about or working for the rights of homosexual people.

In the case of the Saitama prefecture, what would have happened if the author had not learned about the gay magazine? It is reported that 64 percent of homosexual and bisexual men in Japan have damaged their mental health and thought about suicide because of pressure to hide their sexuality (Yamanari, 2001). In Japan, 2,500 young people commit suicide every year and the reasons for 60 percent of these suicides are unclear. It seems certain that some of these deaths were gay youth who could not write a suicide note and committed suicide because of their sexuality and the homophobia in this society. Even if a gay youth wrote a note in which he clarified that his sexuality was the reason for his suicide, his family might hide this fact because both suicide and homosexuality are unwelcome by Japanese society.

In Japanese society, the unwritten presumption is that only heterosexuality is normal; discriminatory expressions against homosexual people are everywhere, including home, school, community, and media. As a result, it is very hard for Japanese gay youth to accept their sexuality (and themselves) when they realize their homosexuality.

Self-disclosure plays an important role when a person wants to be closer to another person. Generally, people gradually become open to others as they develop an intimate relationship. For example, if someone says, "I have a problem" to another person, she or he feels that the person has trusted her or him and may feel more intimate with that person. In this way, disclosing oneself is inevitable to cementing a relationship. However, gay youth often cannot establish intimate friendships because it is difficult for them to disclose their sexuality. It is very important for adolescents to share the idea that they have sexual desire with friends, especially because being sexual is so negatively perceived in our society.

On one hand, through talking about their sexuality and sexual desire with friends, heterosexual teenagers are able to accept their sexual bodies. On the other hand, their sexual bodies bring them sexual pleasure, and it is through sharing a sense of the pleasure that they cement their fraternity. In short, they deepen their friendship by sharing a sense of sin—being sexual and expressing a sense of pleasure— often symbolized by ejaculation.

The following dialogue, from the TV drama *Mito Komon,* is an example of friendships between heterosexual men, as described earlier; in it, the magistrate (prefectural governor in the Edo era) conspires with Echigo-ya (a shopkeeper):

MAGISTRATE: What about Mitsu [a girl whom Magistrate is interested in]?

ECHIGO-YA: Well . . . , I had her wait for you in the next room.

MAGISTRATE: Goooooood! You are cunning.

ECHIGO-YA: Well, yooou, too.

BOTH OF THEM: Hahahahahahaha . . .

Like these two men, heterosexual boys in Japan establish a relationship through a sense of complicity and a common profit through sharing their erotic desire for girls. They eventually accept their (hetero)sexually grown bodies by sharing "sinful and sweet" secrets by exchanging their (hetero)sexual stories and adult books or videos. However, homosexual boys cannot disclose their sexuality and so they cannot live up to their friends' expectations. As a result, it is difficult for them to deepen friendship and fraternity with other boys.

Most schools have homosexual teachers; however, they do not usually disclose their sexuality due to homophobia, and so they are invisible to students. As a result, it is extremely hard for gay youth to imagine their future lives. This has a negative influence on their willingness and energy to live for the future.

REFERENCE

Yamanari, Koji (2001). "64% of Homosexual and Bisexual Have Thought About Committing Suicide." *Mainichi Shimbun* [Osaka newspaper], July 26, p. 2.

Chapter 7

Growing Up Gay in China

Rodge Q. Fann

It was a night four years ago, in my cozy dorm room of a Beijing graduate school. I was chatting with a friend of my roommate. All of a sudden he said to me, "If you were a girl, I would certainly have married you."

To me it was not a surprise at all. I am slightly feminine, soft-spoken, with a delicate style of behavior, and it was the third time a friend had joked about it. The first time was at junior high school eighteen years ago. After I enrolled into a two-year college program, it happened the second time a dozen years ago. Each time I just responded, "Really?" But what I could have said was, "You can still marry me just as I am." To them that was all they saw: a "soft" guy. Most of them had never bothered to pry into why someone might be like that, what would happen to him later, let alone the issue of homosexuality.

I had been a straight A student during most of my school life. That was a perfect shield, discouraging most of my classmates, friends, teachers, and even my family from wondering if there was something "wrong" with this kid. For most Chinese people in the early 1980s, homosexuality was thought of as something immoral. Many people use *Tong Xing Lian,* a Chinese term similar to *homo,* labeling gay men to indicate their disapproval: "A kid like him, he could be a homo? Give me a break." That would be the routine way of thinking about children with excellent grades.

But I am a HOMO.

The author truly appreciates the advice from Mr. Charles R. P. Pouncy and Mr. William Travis, and suggestions from Ms. Juli, in writing this essay.

My first erotic feeling related to men (actually boys) happened when I was in kindergarten in a southeastern province. I forgot what had made me ride on a tough boy's back, but what I remember is that riding on him was so cool! It was my first sense of being gay. It seemed quite natural, but I was a little unclear on the issue at that time. I never had a problem making friends with girls at school with a cute face and terrific grades, and that was another apparent reason why one classmate was shocked when I touched him: "Oh, lord, you're not supposed to be that kind of guy! You have girls around." But overall, most of them didn't seem to mind my hugs, touches, or fondling. And, they *never* related it to the "horrible, horrible fag thing." Most likely, they believed that was the way this soft student expressed friendship.

Even when I was a college student at the end of 1980s, some friends were suspicious about me because I always had male friends around instead of girlfriends. However, what they expressed was pure curiosity rather than hostility. The first time I aggressively kissed another man happened at college. To my great surprise, after an unwillingly short resistance, he eagerly kissed me back and returned my erotic feelings. At that time, we were around twenty.

Until now, I'm still not sure the reason why most of the classmates and friends I've come on to remained positive toward me. Perhaps it was my young and gentle face or maybe they admired me as a very disciplined boy, or both. Certainly most people didn't seem to mind, although some would give me and others such nicknames as "Niang Niang Qiang" (sissy boy), "Jia Ya Tou" (fake girl), or "Da Sao" (big aunt). But most of these were still used in a vague and superficial manner. Other students, especially the tough ones, would scorn me or mimic the way I behaved, which really upset me. Yet they were certain I would get married to a woman and have children. The only difference they recognized was I had a different way of being a boy. Yes, I was still a *boy*. Even in a nasty anonymous letter I got when I was in seventh grade, a girl classmate assumed my heterosexuality, accusing me and another girl classmate of being a nasty couple.

Despite these problems, I did not have many negative experiences growing up gay in China. My worst time was a short period when I temporarily attended classes at another primary school. On my first step into the classroom, I felt tension and hostile feelings from some of the tougher kids. I believe it resulted from my softness and the fact that no one knew anything about me. To them I was simply another easy target. They called me names, spread unwanted nicknames, and mocked me. However, after some exams and praise from different teachers, I received more respectful treatment from my peers. Nevertheless, that short period attending a different school was still horrible. At night, just before sleep, I imagined another day—not a new day, just another day of torture. Yet I genuinely liked the toughest kid there. I had a crush on him, dreaming of riding on his strong back. Later we became friends. Maybe that motivation brought me to school each morning. Or perhaps it explains the saying, "A bad boy is fatal to both pretty girls and to gays."

In Chinese schools excellent grades mean almost everything, no matter if a person is ugly, a sissy, or clumsy at sports. Grades determine most students' fates at school and even further in society. So if a student is good at one or several courses (except physical education) and gets different teachers' praise and support—which means authentic, official confirmation—he or she is the role model of the whole class, the grade, or even the school (which is what happened to me). Without teachers' positive remarks (such as compliments or praise) for a student with poor academic records, an ordinary look, and soft-behaving style, most likely he would become the target of bullying throughout his school life if he also happens to have a weak personality. If a teacher happened to praise him once, it might have saved the student's miserable life. On the contrary, to criticize or mock him would definitely "justify" other students' bullying. Based on what I had experienced, the role of teachers in Chinese classrooms tends to be somewhat critical to a gay student's life.

In my school days, soft-behaving Chinese male students usually were picked on just because they were gendered differently, not because they might be gay. Students did not usually specifically accuse them of being gay. Even though they might call a certain student who was close to another same gender student *homo,* generally it was joking around or making up the issue to show off. For many teenagers in my time, with less impact of propaganda, they did not seem to be disturbed by gay issues that much.

If we examined the sexual history of China, it would be very easy to find Chinese homosexual behavior in every historic period, from emperors to laypersons. Not particular to homosexuality, sex was very natural to the ancient Chinese. As a well-known Chinese saying

goes, "Shi Se Xing Ye" (Appetite for food and sex is nature). Historically, most Chinese have never viewed homosexuality as a crime. It is
simply a gray area most heterosexuals don't pay attention to or even
care about. In ancient times, anal sex with a lower status man was
common. It was simply sex, something that was pursued outside of a
heterosexual lifestyle. You can easily find such accounts in popular
classical novels such as *Hong Lou Meng* (Red mansion dream) and
Jing Pin Mei (Golden vase plum), let alone the erotic novels which
were also very common at that time, like *Pin Hua Bao Jian* (Precious
mirror that ranks flowers). Even today, people who haven't absorbed
the propaganda are tolerant.

My mother's response to my coming out was sort of interesting. As
do many moms, she was always nagging me on the marriage issue,
pushing me to find a girlfriend each time I called home. Then, one
day I responded to her like this: "Don't worry, Mom. Yes, I will get
married in the future." You can imagine the ecstasy she had at that
moment, because I had told her previously that I would never get married but without offering any excuse. So to her it definitely was a huge
change: "Oh, this moment, finally I got a 'yes' from my spoiled son."
I didn't give her much time to feel relieved and continued: "But with
a man." Then it was my turn to be shocked. Rather than give me a
speech or collapse, she said: "You're kidding me! You can play
around [as a gay], but you still have to get married." What my mom
wanted to express was that only a man and a woman can live alone together and take care of each other spiritually. She didn't care about
man-man sex, but she also didn't believe two men could live together
as heterosexual couples do.

Honestly, my mom represents a portion of the open-minded people
in contemporary China who follow the traditional view of sexuality.
But with more than fifty years of propagandistic indoctrination, most
Chinese are not tolerant of nonheterosexuality. Heterosexuality is the
last fortress to stick on the so-called superiority to capitalism banner.
Heteronormativity is the standard and discretion is the expectation. If
everything is done underground or furtively, no public response occurs; if anything brings the gay issue to public attention, it provokes
recrimination and condemnation. In 2001, a gay man in Beijing
stabbed a famous male singer. No one cared whether the singer was
gay, but he claimed he and his friends were robbed by a total stranger.
The "robber," who was later arrested, had a different story. Rumors

began. On an online bulletin board hosted by the Web site *People's Daily* (the newspaper with the highest circulation in China), among thousands of messages posted by people from different walks of life concerning this story, most were virulently homophobic. From these messages you could just feel the hate, anger, and insecurity, but you could not figure out where this hate was coming from, how this anger gathered, and why these individuals felt so insecure. Chinese people don't usually behave like this. Why did they react in this way?

I believe the root of Chinese homophobia is the educational and political propaganda we have experienced for the last fifty years. China and the Chinese have been treated as a single entity for a long time. Therefore, in China, generally there was no concept of individuality unless you were the emperor or the president. At that time, diversity was against "nature": each person had to be the same, from the clothes we wore to the groceries we bought. From the classrooms students sat in to the dictionaries students used, it was about revolution and politics. Despite the open-door policy and economic reform begun twenty years ago, those twisted parts planted deep in the mind have not been reversed completely. In the new socialism with Chinese characteristics, judgment is based on "social morals," focusing on uniformity instead of diversity. Translation: you cannot deviate from the way most people behave, speak, dress, or seek entertainment, even the ways of having sex. In addition, many women think oral sex is so disgusting, dirty, and ugly even just thinking about it is a shame. How do you expect them to react to the gay issue?

The first time I attended a GLBT meeting in the United States, the host asked each one's faith—Christian, Catholic, Islam, etc. When it came to me, jokingly I announced, "Communism." "But that's not even a religion!" someone exclaimed. For most Chinese, it is. From the first grade in primary school to the last year at graduate school, a "political education" course is provided every semester. The newspapers you read, the television shows you watch, the radio programs you listen to are all about communism. So, if your religion is not communism, what is your religion? Or you can declare, "I never believed in communism." But the impact of this kind of education and mass media exposure has already been rooted into your mind, offering the same "individuality" to everyone: intolerance, ignorance, and arrogance. As for the gay issue, this means intolerance of homosexuality, ignorance of gay people, arrogance about being heterosexual. Through years of political education, most people think the same way. Thus, not surprisingly, thousands had railed against the Beijing celebrity. The Internet allowed them to hurl their vicious remarks against gay people.

Although it is used as a weapon to attack gay people, many gay youth and men in China, when they can access the Internet, enjoy surfing on the Web. Before the Internet age, they had to go to such public cruising places as parks, public rest rooms, the woods—which only applied to either the bold or desperate *Tong Zhi* (Chinese term for gay men). Now gay men (mostly young people) can just sit before a computer monitor in his comfy, private home, taking advantage of all that the Internet offers. He can search for "his types" with all kinds of fantasies haunting his mind, or chat with others online claiming, "I'm your Mr. Right," either directly or shyly. And the erotic might also be his favorite surfing content.

Before the Internet age, all information about gay sex had been spread either by friends (if you were lucky to have some gay friends) or, for most gay men, explored through imagination (in which gay men got to be happy; otherwise, they were desperate to become straight in such a conservative country). Now almost all decent gay Web sites present a similar menu: from how to dress sexy to sex positions requiring high skills, from how to pick a one-night stand by astrology signs to what food makes your semen taste bad; in this world *only* gay exists. (Since most Web surfers are young people, almost all materials on gay-related Web sites are for youth.)

Before the Internet age, few gay publications were in circulation. Although there were some very old stories written hundreds years ago and foreign novels such as *Maurice* and *The Thief's Journal,* these only made you regret being in China at this moment in history. Now everyone could post whatever he wants to express in any gay Web site as long as he spends some time to write and has some feelings to share. *Lan Yu,* the first gay movie of China, was released in 2001. Adapted from a novel that first appeared on the Internet, it is a story about the ten-year love between a poor college student and a new bourgeoisie set in Beijing. Of course, gay Chinese can also supplement their information with more Western views on GLBT issues, including reports about gay conferences, movie reviews, parade descriptions, celebrity tabloids—and don't forget capitalist pornography. Now there are many means for Chinese gay youth to hook up with the same type of friends, whether for a one-night stand or a long-term relationship. But outside of cyberspace everything remains secretive and furtive. However, what we have right now is still great progress when compared ten years ago without the thin phone line and a small box called a modem.

The era of China's economic reform is the clear dividing line for most people when it comes to gay issues. Before these reforms every person was supposed to be identical; any deviation—but especially sexual deviation—was a taboo. Now it's a little better to be gay and attend school in China. With the open-door policy implemented deeply and widely, more Western culture is available through movies, TV shows, books, music, art, and other commodities. Students who have neither developed inhibitions in their minds nor accepted clichés from the propaganda have been the first to absorb it. Thus, when I was at graduate school in Beijing three years ago, to most of my classmates whether I was a gay or not was just like a piece of translucent paper between me and them. If I let it stay there, no one broke it; if I removed the paper, they recognized it all of a sudden: "Yes, he is!" No one panicked as long as I didn't hit on anyone. But if I fell for somebody, even though he was gay, he would still get furious. It's insulting. It's immoral to most people still—although they do not care what gay people do. They believe they have a higher moral standard just sticking to heterosexuality. No one wants to carry a bad name, even though it's not bad at all.

In summer of 2002 I returned to China and stayed in Shanghai, the country's biggest and most prosperous city. Strolling on the busiest street, Nanjing Road, a slender man approached my American friend and me, offering, "Wanna girl?" Yes, in English. On another part of the same road, a young man leaning against a pole ogled my friend, singing, "Heyyyyyyyy, Daddyyyy," again in English. I just joked with him, "Hey, you got lots of choices here." Just four years earlier I was caught by the police when sitting on a man's thighs at midnight in a cruising place in Beijing. Now you can hook up with anyone you want on the street! And with the Internet becoming more and more popular, quick setup, 419 (a colloquial expression meaning "for one night," derived from the similarity in pronunciation), quick breakup, and another quick setup is the routine for many gay Chinese youth today. Maybe because many of them have been restrained so long, the libido inside of them has been accumulated for so long, they desperately want to let it out. Just let it out. Have a look at the bathhouses, gay bars/clubs, and cruising places. It is not difficult to figure out what's going on there. Many of them don't care about AIDS (acquired immunodeficiency syndrome). It sounds distant: only debauched Americans get it. We're just beginning, not yet. Sound familiar? Remind you of the 1970s? Yes, many of them are just repeating what America did thirty years ago. The only difference is with the Internet China is moving faster than its predecessor. China is dealing with gay issues, teenage sex, abortion, drug use, adolescent crime, adultery, changing spouses, sex parties, you name it. To educators and policymakers in China, it's really a good idea to learn what America has done to curb different sorts of social problems, especially in young people. Since it's still in the beginning, it should be easier to nip it in the bud before it gets frenzied.

Chinese are still Chinese. No matter how sex-starved some of us look on the outside, how vulgarly some of us chat online, most of us are still searching for our soul mates. Most Chinese still value family, true love, human morals. These also exist in the hearts of most Chinese gay youth. Internet gay stories, however, focus on one theme: getting hurt but still searching. Most take place on campus and are based on true experiences. These young gays struggle to find their real identity yet have no time to enjoy it. They still have to pretend, cracking straight jokes, sharing scorn at "homos," and then going underground or online to find their true love in a now material world. "I wanna have sex with, and only with, my soul mate," a gay youth may declare. "But how to find him? It seems everyone just wants to have sex and then wave good-bye." Love *and* sex disturbs young gays in contemporary China. They can find such free publications as *Peng You* (Friends), a pamphlet about safe sex and gay issues at gay bars or any gay-friendly place, but what they really need are role models—real gay models close to them, to encourage them, to lead them—and love *with* sex.

Economic reforms and the Internet have made it easy for gay youth to identify themselves and enjoy it a little bit. But growing up gay and living as a gay person in China are still underground issues. At schools in China, teachers have a unique role in shaping teenagers' minds. If they can begin to teach diversity and tolerance in sexual orientation, it would be of great help not only to gay youth but also to the majority of heterosexuals to break through the gay clichés.

Chapter 8

Commentaries

Here, several distinguished educators with various backgrounds and from different countries were asked to comment following their reading of these two essays. Given space limitations, these are more evocative than particulate, but collectively they provide multiple platforms for reflection. Their commentaries are followed by similarly brief concluding remarks from Mr. Ashito and Mr. Fann.

One should be aware of the rich tradition of homosexuality (and bisexuality) in these two societies—and the harmful influence of the West in altering this tradition. In Japan, a literary tradition is found as early as the eighth century publication of *The Chronicles of Japan*, describing the love of two male courtiers. There, too, is the classic *Tale of Genji*, written three centuries later, and Ihara Saikaku's *The Great Mirror of Male Love*, a collection of short stories celebrating homosexuality within the samurai class and in the Kabuki theater (Carpenter, 1914).

Similarly, a tradition exists in Chinese literature (e.g., *The Book of Odes*) as well as its social history. For example, throughout the four hundred years of the Han dynasty (that began in 206 B.C.), homosexuality was found among its emperors and within the fashion-conscious imperial court system. The most famous was perhaps Emperor Ai whose failed attempt to hand over his crown to Dong Xian resulted in the lover's suicide and the end of that dynasty. Their devoted relationship was signified as the "passion of the cut sleeve" due to Emperor Ai's decision to cut his sleeve on which his lover slept rather than awaken him (Hinsch, 1990; Samshasa, 1984).

No native Japanese or Chinese religions have singled out homosexuality for condemnation, although both countries have felt the impact of Western religion—and other forms of colonization. It was in Japan's Meiji Period (mid-nineteenth century to early twentieth), for example, that in seeking Western approval antihomosexual attitudes in schools (and, for a brief period, in the law) were stressed, with an even greater enforcement of heterodoxy during America's post–World War II occupation (Churchill, 1967; Schalow, 1990). Even in relatively tolerant China (despite earlier neo-Confucian moralism), the twentieth century emulation of Western science and restructuring of Chinese marriage (exacerbated by the communist regime) ended centuries of general tolerance (Ruan and Yang-mei, 1988).

Today, given the importance of the family in both societies, homosexuality is often subsumed under or within the institution of marriage (as in the case of Japanese novelist Mishima Yukio, whose heterosexual marriage was only slightly better known than his homosexual activity). It is also being subjected to another wave of Westernization—this time under the aegis of gay liberation. As noted by some commentators here and elsewhere (e.g., Altman, 2001; Connell, 1999; Cruz-Malave and Manalansan IV, 2002), this globalization of gay culture (and identity) coupled with the categorization and commodification of desire create strange bedfellows for those of us seeking an end to homophobia but also struggling with Western cultural hegemony.

In each of these essays, a nearly classic theme of the individual versus society shines through. Although set in Asia, the authors' struggles mirror those I have heard from LGBT young people in America, many of whom face similar barriers when seeking support, information, and affirmation. I would imagine that most LGBT Americans would find these writings not very "foreign" at all. One interesting distinction was that good grades seem to have shielded one author from antigay harassment, whereas for American gay males academic achievement often brings further scorn as evidence that they are not "real men." Otherwise, the themes of the stories seem remarkably similar to narratives written by LGBT youth in the United States.

In fact, that in itself is not a surprise, as the "gay identity" most of the authors ascribe or aspire to often seems to be one accessed from Western or Western-influenced sources, including the Internet and print publications. Both writers described "finding" themselves via these sources. These sources seem to give the authors a conceptual framework to understand their same-sex desires, and language to talk about it, which they had lacked before.

This raises an interesting question: Is the hostility the authors face founded primarily in homophobia or due to cultural differences? Same-sex behavior is hardly "foreign" to Chinese and Japanese cultures, and the historic record shows that it has been a well-documented and well-known phenomenon in those societies for millennia. What is new in the authors' stories is a different construction and understanding of that experience, borrowed, as noted, largely from Western sources. Rooted in a Western value system that places a premium on individual self-expression, this construct inspires hostility from Chinese and Japanese traditionalists, as these societies have often expected individual identities to be subordinated in favor of highly proscribed social roles and the larger group identity. The fact that the Chinese author links things "getting better" for Chinese gays to the spread of Western concepts of cultural and economic individualism reveals this connection. We must then ask: Is the hostility the authors encounter caused by their interest in same-sex sexual behavior or is it due to the "gay identity" they have borrowed from Western sources to construct and then express that desire? I suspect the latter is as much the root of the conflict as the former.

As globalization continues to spread the Western gospel of individualism and its attendant construction of gay identity around the globe, it will be interesting to see how such questions of identity are resolved in non-Western societies. Will new constructions of the gay experience emerge from these cultural encounters or will all be assimilated into a dominant model that comes from the West? These selections seem to indicate the latter trend will dominate. Just as McDonald's and Kentucky Fried Chicken have replaced sushi and dim sum in the diets of many young Japanese and Chinese, it seems that traditional constructions of same-sex behavior taken from the samurai and imperial ages are being displaced by Western ones that prize coming out and living outside the institution of heterosexual marriage as time wears on, based on the work of these authors. Whether this is a good or a bad thing, I leave to the reader to decide.

Kevin Jennings
Executive Director, GLSEN
New York City

As I sit here writing in the blistering midsummer heat of New Zealand, it's interesting (but probably not that surprising) to find that the narratives of the young Japanese and Chinese gay men connect strongly to my hybrid life as both an academic and as a researcher working in schools on sexuality/gender and diversity issues. These stories, situated as they are in a very different cultural context, speak to me.

The young men's stories provide a powerful justification for thoughtful and considered research in schools that acknowledges the complex and shifting intersections of sexuality, ethnicity, gender, and class—both in terms of the ways that students (and teachers) constitute their identities, and also in terms of social practices within schools (Davies, 1996).

Even more than that (and this is the challenging part within the functionalist cultures of schools!), the narratives illustrate the need for research which works toward acknowledging and addressing ways that teachers in the classroom, and schools generally, have a role in exploring intersections of diversity within particular cultural contexts.

The narratives that the young gay men have written powerfully convey the intense challenges involved in negotiating the minefield of what it means to grow up as young gay men within a powerfully heteronormative cultural context. It is valuable for me to understand how complex interrelationships between sexuality/gender/ethnicity and class are played out for the writers, and also the powerful way that the particular positionalities affect the writer's lives.

And yet, despite the immense juggling feat that both of the writers undergo in order to negotiate the complexities of their lives, they find ways to survive and sometimes even to thrive. Popular culture rather than schooling processes appear to play a defining role in enabling the writers to have some sense of well-being in relation to their sexuality.

So how can these complexities and their lived consequences be shifted, and what's the role of schools in that process? Well, that's another juggling act. The challenge seems to me to somehow hold on to the complexities of what diversity means in specific cultural contexts (and their lived realities), understand and acknowledge the constraints that need to be negotiated to develop and try strategies (as Fann does so well), and yet still maintain some forward momentum in developing and testing strategies in schools that put addressing intersections of diversity at the forefront of teaching, learning, and schooling practices. I call this "informed action" (Quinlivan, Under Review). Kusher (in Lather, 1997) describes it more evocatively as "non stupid optimism."

It would be difficult and challenging work within China and Japan, and it's tricky work in New Zealand as well. My experiences as a researcher working in several secondary schools over the past year on a pilot gender and diversity project with teachers in schools in a New Zealand context confirm that schools have a long way to go in addressing student diversity. Some teachers don't see this task as part of their role or the role of schools (Quinlivan, Under Review). Others are nervous about legitimating what they consider to be dangerous knowledge inherent in acknowledging gendered and sexual diversities (Britzman, 1998).

However, encouraging signs are emerging in my corner of the world. The New Zealand Ministry of Education is placing an increasing emphasis on the role of social outcomes in education and, perhaps more significantly, is prepared to sink more resources into a second phase of the gender and diversity project. Another New Zealand researcher is making some significant progress in "deprogramming" secondary teachers so that they can see building relationships with students as an integral part of their role in meeting the needs of Maori students in mainstream secondary schools (Bishop, Richardson, and Tiakiwai, 2002).

Hearing the stories that tell of the lived realities of young gay Chinese and Japanese young men and understanding the wider cultural constraints that they live within is the first step in beginning the challenging work of moving toward reculturing the heteronormative educational contexts that they have had to negotiate.

Kathleen Quinlivan
Research Associate, Education Department
University of Canterbury

Is homophobia culture specific? Reading these stories by troubled teens, it all sounds so terribly well known. In so many research studies, personal stories, and anecdotes, we are confronted with the same kind of complaints by LGBT teenagers. They are isolated and lonely; they feel depressed and worthless; they have difficulty finding love and understanding; when they finally find some sex, it is often in a context or personal frenzy that could lead to abuse or STDs (sexually transmitted diseases), apart from the mental unsettlement. No wonder they often say that a supporting role model saved their life!

These stories made me consider whether homophobia or homo-negativity is specific to cultures or a global phenomenon. Both Akihiko Komiya and Rodge Fann seem to point toward the specific contexts in Japan and China, but I cannot stop thinking about how similar the stories of all young people sound, how similar their problems seem to be all over the world.

Many scholars have shown that the concept of homosexuality and even the word itself is a European one, and even a quite recent invention as well. In such constructionist accounts, they stress that many forms and shapes of same-sex behavior exist and can change over time. What consequence does this have for our thinking about what to do about the problems of LGBT teenagers? Why do I experience a rift between the stories here and the scholarly exposés about the historical concepts of LGBT (non)identity?

It occurred to me that maybe the solution does not rest in the definition of homosexuality but in homophobia. Same-sex behavior may come in many shapes, but negative feelings toward people who do not conform to social and sexual norms are much more standard. Even in cultures in which certain forms of same-sex behavior were more or less accepted, it usually was taboo, secret, or looked upon ambiguously by the general population. Almost everywhere, I regret to say, the social norm to act out heterosexual behavior or to comply to heterosexual rituals made any other emotion of behavior difficult. With the cultural imperialism of the European/North American nations, a specific kind of heterosexual norms seems to have taken a central and global role. In the current globalization, this norm is becoming so general that it is nowadays difficult to say whether this is a culture-specific thing or just a local version of the same global heterosexism.

When we are dealing with the same general kind of homophobia all over the world, could we not combat it in one way while working together? In 1997, during the Amsterdam Gay Games and in collaboration with Amnesty International and HIVOS (International Humanist Institute for Cooperation with Developing Countries), I organized an international workshop on education about LGBT issues in schools. I think it was the first time something like that happened. Before we started the initiative, we expected such education to be very different in all parts of the world. However, when we finally did the workshop and representatives from Latin America, the United States, Canada, Europe, Africa, and Asia attended, we found many similarities. In most cases, educational and awareness sessions were done by volunteers of local LGBT organizations. They tell their personal stories and answer any questions students might have. Students tend to have a lot of questions. They know the subject is taboo and an awareness session by LGBT people is one of the few opportunities young people have to get to know more about something they find intriguing. Throughout the world, the questions asked by (mostly heterosexual) students are more or less the same: How did you discover your same-sex feelings? Did you tell others about them? How did your parents react? How do you deal with discrimination? How do you meet a partner? Who is the male and the female in your relationship?

Of course, many of these questions are tainted by prejudice. Students are so indoctrinated with the heterosexual norm that any different feeling, choice, or lifestyle creates revulsion or at the least surprise. But the curiosity of the students and the open minds of the educators offer huge opportunities to discuss things.

My conclusion is that we can learn much from combating homophobia on the operational level of group discussions. Cultural differences will come into the discussion because students will refer to religion or tradition as the reason for their homophobia. However, when we take a closer look, it seems the homophobia is more based in personal revulsion and negative attitudes that are based on a norm of heterosexuality. Young people have learned only one acceptable way to have sex and relationships: a public heterosexual one. Anything different is unknown and soon becomes the unwanted, the strange, and the fearful. On this more abstract level (well, in the classroom it is not so abstract), cultural differences suddenly seem less relevant.

This is not to say no differences exist. During the workshop, it became clear that although the group discussions tended to be more or less the same, the way to get into schools and other public organizations was often very different. In Northern Europe, LGBT organizations have gained such social acceptance that they can write letters to schools and offer to carry out awareness sessions. Some teachers see the offer as a useful exercise to add to the effect of their human rights curriculum. About 10 percent of the schools in the Netherlands invite the local LGBT organization to conduct some sessions every year. In Brazil, such acceptance is on the rise, but still the LGBT organizations get themselves invited only by offering a complete AIDS-prevention curriculum. In this context, they teach the students to talk more openly about sex and, toward the end of the course, about such issues as homosexuality and being transgender. In the more progressive places in Africa, we see a similar strategy. In most Muslim cultures, discussing sex in mixed groups is almost impossible due to social constraints and shame that the culture instills on the students. So the isolated attempts we find for education are in the shape of street corner work regarding AIDS or prostitution. In Asia, too, getting into schools is still impossible for LGBT educators. However, here human and sexual rights might provide an opportunity.

Peter Dankmeijer
Director, Empowerment Lifestyle Services
Amsterdam

What clear strong voices Akihiko Komiya and Rodge Fann sound in these autobiographical reflections on being gay in Japan and China. Despite the difficulties of being gay in these countries (different from each other and yet the same and recognizable to many of us older queers in the West), there appears to be movement in the glacier of heterosexism. Such movement is evident in Fann's narrative, as he reports private indifference to (if public disapproval of) queer desire in China. From actual communities we flee to virtual ones: cyberspace.

In Japan, it may be evident in those Japanese comics in which, according to Sandra Buckley (1991), androgynous figures are drawn wrapped in each other's arms, naked in bed, passionately making love, gazing longingly into each other's eyes, and kissing each other on the cheek. These images of young lovers kissing are within the bishonen genre. A scene of a man kissing another man on the lips is portrayed as being "more sensuous than any bed scene" (Buckley, 1991, p. 175).

The word *jiyu* (freedom), Buckley notes, occurs again and again in the pages of the bishonen comics. The feature story of the July 1989 edition is headlined "All My Life" and follows the gradual shift of the old male protagonist's love from his girlfriend to a beautiful young boy.

By the 1980s, Buckley tells us, the market for the bishonen comics had expanded far beyond the original readership of pubescent schoolgirls. Now it included gay men and women, heterosexual male university students, and young heterosexual women, in particular young *okusan* (housewives—literally "the person at the back of the house"). The bishonen comics would seem to represent a denial of (hetero)sexuality among teenage girls, but such a reading risks denying, Buckley suggests, the sexual awareness and curiosity of the millions of teenage girls who purchase these comics.

What is being denied or rejected by the readership of the bishonen comics is the strict regulation of gender and sexual practice in postwar Japanese society, despite the difficulties encountered by Akihiko Komiya and the narratives of his fellow queer youth. (Did they read these comics?) The bishonen comics offer young men "a fantastical space for the exploration of sexual desire outside the closed circuit of the oedipal theater of the family but on the familiar territory of the homosocial formations of their youth" (Buckley, 1991, p. 180). Such homosocial formations, she continues, structure the social relationships of Japanese men throughout their lives—echoes of the mythology of the "comrade samurai" lived out in the contemporary workplace.

These comics *(manga)* functioned, Buckley (1991) speculates, to transform events associated with everyday experience—she lists commuting, eating, golf clubs, tea ceremony utensils, baseball bats, food processors, secretaries, bosses, plumbers, and much more—into eroticized objects of fantasy. In the Edo period, woodblock prints of the phallus were everywhere, she reports.

In contemporary Japanese pornographic comic books the penis does not appear; it is nowhere. Yet it is everywhere. The penis is present in its absence. The current legal requirement that the penis be absent has led, according to Buckley, to graphic innovations that communicate the Lacanian idea that the phallus is not equal to the penis. The phallus, in Lacan and in these Japanese comic books, transcends the anatomical, signifying the power that is the privilege of the creature whose identity is inseparable from that organ.

Kaja Silverman (1992, p. 6) quotes Slavoj Zizek (1989, p. 118) to suggest that fantasy not only "provides the co-ordinates of our desire," but "constructs the frame enabling us to desire something." Through fantasy, then "we learn 'how to desire.'" If, through comics, homosexual desire circulates among "straight" readers, how "straight" can they be? Can that queer cyberspace that Fann narrates and that queer "homosocial" desire evident in Komiya's depiction of the TV drama *Mito Komon* be kept segregated in virtual reality? Does the "fear of a queer planet" foreshadow the actuality of a queer planet?

William F. Pinar
St. Bernard Parish Alumni Endowed Professor
Louisiana State University

Most of what the young writers from Japan and China write about resonates with my experiences of young people in Zimbabwe and other parts of Africa. It seems that no matter where you are in the world, universal experiences are associated with growing up gay or lesbian in conservative, heterosexist communities: self-denial, self-hatred, loneliness, thoughts of suicide, family pressure to marry and conform to the norm, peer-group pressure, and rejection by friends. There are also the yearnings for companionship, love, affection—and the need to share experiences with like-minded people. These are the same general themes found in letters by young people when they first make contact with the Gays and Lesbians of Zimbabwe (GALZ).

Although China has adopted a more progressive open-door policy toward influences from the West and Japan is heavily influenced by American materialism, both are still highly conformist societies. But despite the taboos surrounding LGBT issues—which extend to official silence within the school system—young people find ways to make contact with one another and they manage to thrive. The cultural climate in Zimbabwe may be very different, but the underlying conservatism and the official government disapproval are much the same. Young gay Zimbabweans will recognize the Chinese student's description of propaganda during the Cultural Revolution: that homosexuality is a foreign perversion which has infiltrated from the West. In the case of Zimbabwe, it has been described to as "the white man's disease" riding on the bandwagon of so-called human rights. It is supposedly taught to young people in an attempt to destabilize the nation. Young gay and lesbian people are said to be in the pay of whites.

Rodge Q. Fann points to homosexual themes in ancient Chinese literature as proof that same-sex love is neither new nor imported. This is more difficult in Zimbabwe which, until colonialism, had no written records. When Canadian historian Marc Epprecht (1998) unearthed in the National Archives more than 250 court cases involving sexual relations between black Africans from 1892 (when the Victorian courts opened in Southern Rhodesia) to 1923, his evidence was expected to carry much weight, demonstrating that homosexuality is indigenous to this part of the world. As in China, historical evidence has been simply ignored because it has not fit with the principles of the newly invented nationalist culture.

The major difference between China and Japan on one hand and Zimbabwe on the other is that although there are no gay-affirmative government policies in the first two countries, in Zimbabwe homophobia has been purposefully politicized and placed squarely on the national agenda. Lesbian and gay people are banned from speaking about themselves on television and radio; only antigay propaganda is permitted. Nevertheless, as in China, life for the LGBT community here is emerging. There are no gay clubs or bars as such, but young gay people are mostly well tolerated by young people. In some clubs it is even fashionable to be seen associating with the gay clientele. The fact that GALZ exists openly and is able to advertise in the independent press and in the phone directory is a big step forward from 1970s Rhodesia when the police consistently raided and closed the clubs. Although use of the Internet is still limited, especially in rural areas, it is fast becoming one of the major tools used by young people to learn about gay and lesbian life in other parts of the world and to make contact with the outside.

Not surprisingly, the letter writer in Japan exhibits no concerns about American influence on Japanese society. Rodge Q. Fann, on the other hand, is more wary of the pitfalls of adopting American-style gay values wholesale. Many of us have similar fears in Zimbabwe. We have consciously avoided encouraging a gay-ghetto mentality here: family is vital and it is difficult to survive in this country if your family turns its back on you. Largely, this has to do with matters of economic independence. Richer gay and lesbian people have the choice of whether they wish to move away from home; in Zimbabwe, where most young gay people are poor and many unemployed, moving away from home is not a viable option. It has always been GALZ's policy to find ways in which to reintegrate young lesbian and gay people back into their families.

Keith Goddard
Coordinator of the Gays and Lesbians
of Zimbabwe

REFERENCES

Altman, D. (2001). Global gaze/global gays. In J. Hawley (Ed.), *Postcolonial and queer theories* (pp. 1-18). Westport, CT: Greenwood.

Bishop, R., Richardson, C., and Tiakiwai, S. (2002). Effective teaching for Maori students in medium and mainstream settings. Paper presented at the Researching with Others: Crossing the Divides, Bridging Research, Building Relationships Conference, July 2002, Waipapa Marae, The University of Auckland, Auckland, Aotearoa/New Zealand.

Britzman, D. (1998). *Lost subjects, contested objects: Toward a psychoanalytic inquiry of learning.* New York: State University of New York Press.

Buckley, S. (1991). "Penguin in bondage": A graphic tale of Japanese comic books. In C. Penley and A. Ross (Eds.), *Technoculture* (pp. 163-195). Minneapolis: University of Minnesota Press.

Carpenter, E. (1914). The Samurai of Japan. In E. Carpenter, *Intermediate types among primitive folk* (pp. 137-160). New York: Kennerley.

Churchill, W. (1967). *Homosexual behavior among males: A cross-cultural and cross-species investigation.* New York: Hawthorn.

Connell, R. (1999). Sex in the world. In D. Epstein and J. Sears (Eds.), *A dangerous knowing* (pp. 89-101). London: Cassell.

Cruz-Malave, A. and Manalansan IV, M. (Eds.) (2002). *Queer globalizations: Citizenship and the afterlife of colonialism.* New York: New York University Press.

Davies, B. (1996*). Power, knowledge, desire: Changing school organization and management practices.* Canberra, Australia: Department of Employment, Education, and Youth Affairs.

Epprecht, M. (1998). "Good God almighty. What's this!" Homosexual "crime" in early colonial Zimbabwe. In S. Murray and W. Roscoe (Eds.), *Boy-wives and female husbands* (pp. 197-220). New York: St. Martin's Press.

Hinsch, B. (1990). *Passions of the cut sleeve: The male homosexual tradition in China.* Berkeley: University of California Press.

Lather, P. (1997). Working the ruins of feminist ethnography: Toward economies of responsibility and possibility. Paper presented at the American Educational Research Association Conference, Chicago, April.

Quinlivan, K. (under review). Analysis and action: A model for exploring intersections of gender and diversity in six New Zealand secondary schools. *Gender and Education.*

Ruan, F. and Yang-mei, T. (1988). Male homosexuality in contemporary Mainland China. *Archives of Sexual Behavior, 17,* 189-199.

Samshasha (1984). *History of homosexuality in China.* Hong Kong: Pink Triangle Press.

Schalow, P. (1990). Japan. In W. Dynes (Ed.), *Encyclopedia of homosexuality* (pp. 32- 636). New York: Garland.

Silverman, K. (1992). *Male subjectivity at the margins.* New York: Routledge.

Zizek, S. (1989). *The sublime of object of ideology.* London: Verso.

Chapter 9

Authors' Reactions

"From actual communities we flee to virtual ones: cyberspace," writes William F. Pinar. What a pointed comment. For many Chinese gay youth, gay bars/clubs are luxury places beyond their affordability: forty *yuan* (about five dollars) for a glass of beer. Furthermore, cruising places and bathhouses are too risky and sexually explicit with the possibility of being raided. Thus, the Internet is the perfect world: for talking to another gay, chat online; for viewing news on gay movements all over the globe, visit gay Web sites; for reading gay romance, click the story section; for having sex, try cybersex.

The Internet liberates the whole generation of gay youth who are still in the closet. In this cyber world, you don't feel lonely anymore. You don't have to deny yourself since so much virtual fun is available. You don't hate yourself, feel marriage pressure any longer—as long as you didn't get kicked offline. As computer games become a new addiction to many straight teenagers (certainly gay youth like them, too), cyberspace is paradise for many Chinese young gay people.

However, the Internet is also a double-edged sword. Promoting positive and helpful gay knowledge, the Internet is also the inspection-free media for erotica. When I was in China in the summer of 2002, a teenager asked my advice whether he should listen to his mother's lecture about not getting online at all or using it only for study. Here, no one can keep away from the erotic content in cyberspace, especially young people, which is the major concern of most parents. Encouraging this young man to take full advantage of the Internet for learning, I honestly pointed out he had to curb himself of the sexually explicit material. To an adolescent student, it's natural to be curious about sex. Rather than restrain them in a nonsexual, neutral world, becoming informed is human. A limited portion of pornography is a vivid form of sexual education, but if an individual can't extricate himself or herself from Web erotica, it is just another form of teen suicide. Not being able to find regular sources to release their desires as their straight friends do, many gay youth love this virtual world. Not surprisingly, when they return to the real world only disappointment awaits them. They hate reality more and soon go back to virtual reality. Eventually, gay youth have to face reality and deal with real people; what is left for them, as Keith Goddard writes, is more "self-denial, self-hatred, loneliness."

Hooking up online is another facet of cyber world. Without any chance to post personal ads on major Chinese media or to join a party competing for a date with "Joe Millionaire" or a "bachelorette" (even American LGBT youth have no chance—yet), personal profiles on the Internet are free, safe, convenient, and accurate. At least they are supposed to be. But that's a tricky issue.

No one wants to be a loser; everyone longs for his prince. Not surprisingly, perfect guys are everywhere—in the cyber world. Sharp eyes are useless; sharp minds are needed to read into every line. But many gay youth lack these skills or fail to use common sense. There was a strange murder case in the province of Taiwan about two years ago. A quiet college student's body was found abandoned in the suburbs. When police searched his personal computer, they concluded his murder was the result of his first blind S&M date with a person he met online. The virtual and the real collided.

Rodge Q. Fann*

As some people comment, same-sex intimate relationships in premodern Japan have and had been well known. They have been referenced at home and abroad with surprise and/or praise many times. But we need to be aware that they have been referred to by *certain* sorts of people. I'm under the impression that there are two kinds.

One kind is Japanese heterosexual intellectuals (though in most cases they don't seem intellectual) who know that male-male relationships were well accepted and even considered noble in Japan. It sometimes seems these homophobes want to show off their knowledge on pederasty in premodern Japan from their privileged perspective to imply their being generous enough to accept some sort of homo-

*The author truly appreciates the advice from Mr. Charles R. P. Pouncy and Mr. William Travis, and suggestions from Ms. Juli in writing this essay.

sexuality. We (Japanese gay youth) have to be careful of this within academia.

The other kind is some Western gay men. They project their wish to be liberated upon Japanese old days' code of intimacy between male bodies, which was not at all oppressed. If my interpretation is correct, it is one way that Orientalism constructs the "Asian mystique." We also have to beware of Orientalism in the field of education and gay studies around the globe.

The love of the samurai and *chigo* in premodern Japan is often expressed as Japanese homosexuality and a love between a boy and a gay man. It is certain that those were same-*sex* relationships, but not necessarily same-*gender* relationships. From the present perspective, the love of the samurai might be called "fraternal homosociality with physical contact" and the love of the *chigo* might be called "sexual substitutes for Buddhist monks who were prohibited from having sex with women."

In the 1910s and 1920s, Japan imported Western sexology, which labeled same-gender love as abnormal sexual desire (Oda, 1996). Thereafter, "(abnormal) homosexuality" has been constructed and degraded in Japan. It was not until the early 1970s that the first commercial gay magazine, *Bara-zoku,* was published by a heterosexual editor. In those days, many homosexual men still internalized this psychiatric code, originally imported from the West and uncritically accepted until 1995 by the Japanese Psychiatric Association; they also suffered from internalized homophobia. In the mid-1980s, the advent of AIDS finally brought the advent of Japanese gay men (no longer "homos") who organized and acted to stop AIDS and to tackle homophobia. Since then, the gay liberation movement has speedily and steadily been established.

At the turn of the twenty-first century, these efforts have bore fruit in the public arena. In 2000, the Tokyo Metropolitan Government included homosexuals under its human rights protection policy. And it was recently reported that ten home economics textbooks out of nineteen will describe a same-gender couple as a family form (*Buddy,* 2003). Since nearly all textbooks have to be approved (and usually censored) by the Ministry of Education and Science and because teaching is based on those textbooks, this action will have an immeasurable influence on students.

Japan is a relatively uniform and homogeneous country. On one hand, because of this we have been ignored and ostracized. But on the other hand, once the pendulum begins to swing toward the gay-affirmative side, sudden changes may be expected.

I am subject to gay identity (and English language); queer theorists (and Esperantists) may laugh at me. But as Japanese theorist Fushimi (2001) points out, the label *gay* paradoxically brings oppression to gay men but also provides an effective network of men who are sexually attracted to other men. Kevin Jennings says, "it will be interesting to see how such questions of identity are resolved in non-Western societies." In the Japanese gay movement, overall gay identity has been playing a positive role. Though some Japanese queer theorists (most of them heterosexual) had been rather loud against gay identity, since one gay theorist Noguchi (2000) has refuted Butler's (1990) and Halperin's (1990) theories, these Japanese theorists have been queerly quiet.

As Japanese, we have been good at importing anything; not only sexology, gay liberation, and queer theory, but also dim sum, Chinese medicine, and Chinese characters. Where do we Japanese gay youth drift with a flood of imported items? God, Buddha, and Allah know!

Akihiko Komiya

REFERENCES

Butler, J. (1990). *Gender trouble.* New York: Routledge.

Fushimi, N. (2001). Atorakushon to shite no gei no rogo [Gay men's aging as attraction]. *Keiso-Shobo [Queer Japan],* 5, pp. 39-43.

Halperin, D. (1990). *One hundred years of homosexuality and other essays on Greek love.* New York: Routledge.

Noguchi, K. (2000). Kuiarion to posutokozoshugi [Queer theory and post-structuralism]. *Keiso-Shobo [Queer Japan],* 3, pp. 192-219.

Oda, M. (1996). *Sei.* Tokyo: Sansei-Do.

"Tera-Shuppan" (2003, March). *Buddy* 10(3), p. 44.

SECTION II:
RESEARCH AND POLICY

Chapter 10

School Experiences of Gay, Lesbian, Bisexual, and Transgender Youth

Sarah E. Holmes
Sean Cahill

Gay, lesbian, bisexual, and transgender (GLBT) youth are coming out younger, on average at age sixteen (Herdt and Boxer, 1996, as cited in Human Rights Watch, 2001). Many become dangerously isolated—rejected by family and friends, harassed and attacked by their peers in school, and demeaned by society. Because of their youth, many lack independent resources and may have a hard time accessing support. This problem is accentuated for GLBT youth of color who already face social prejudice and stigmatization because of race or ethnicity. By coming out, they also risk rejection by their community of origin and, therefore, intensified isolation (Ryan and Futterman, 1998; Varney, 2001). Children of GLBT parents are also commonly targeted and harassed by peers in much the same ways as GLBT youth.

GLBT youth and children of GLBT parents can experience intense harassment and violence, but even with little support they often display amazing strength, resiliency, and self-advocacy. In many instances, GLBT youth have organized to demand and effect changes in policy to make schools safer. Increasingly, students, educators, administrators, activists, researchers, and policymakers are turning their attention to the school experiences of GLBT youth. They are working to better understand and challenge the frequent harassment

Editing and research assistance provided by Michelle Agostini, Mitra Ellen, Rachel Hill, and Ruth McFarlane. Generous funding was provided by the Kevin J. Mossier Foundation.

63

and violence many youth experience as well as the impact on their mental and physical health. In response, GLBT youth and other advocates have spearheaded successful intervention programs, including nondiscrimination and antiharassment policies, antihomophobia initiatives, community, and school-based support groups offering GLBT students education and positive peer interaction, and adult mentors programs.

This review begins with an overview of what is known about the experiences of GLBT youth and children of GLBT parents in the school setting.

HOW MANY GLBT YOUTH ARE THERE?

It is difficult to determine exactly how many GLBT, school-aged youth there are in the United States. The answer may lie, in part, in how GLBT youth is defined. Published studies vary in how they define and determine sexual orientation in their samples; self-identification, reported sexual experiences, and responses related to romantic attraction or fantasies are among the methods used to determine the percentage of gay, lesbian, and bisexual youth (Savin-Williams, 2001b).

In the 1987 Minnesota Adolescent Health Survey, 1.1 percent of teenagers described themselves as bisexual or homosexual, and 5.1 percent reported same-sex attraction or anticipated future same-sex sexual experience (Mortimer, 1987). The 1991 U.S. National American Indian Adolescent Health Survey of youth in reservation schools found only 1.6 percent of respondents self-identified as gay or bisexual, but 4.4 percent reported same-sex attraction or anticipated future same-sex experience (U.S. Department of Health and Human Services, 1991). In the 1997 Massachusetts Youth Risk Behavior Survey (YRBS), more than 4 percent of respondents either self-identified as gay or bisexual or reported same-sex sexual experience (Goodenow, 1997). In Vermont's 1997 YRBS, 5.4 percent of young men and 3.4 percent of young women reported same-sex sexual activity (Vermont Department of Health, 1997). In Seattle's 1995 Teen Health Risk Survey, 4.5 percent said they were lesbian, gay, or bisexual, and another 4 percent said they were "not sure" of their sexual orientation (Seattle Public Schools, 1996).

Although we don't know exactly how many U.S. students are gay, lesbian, or bisexual, these studies indicate that about 1 million of the nation's 15 million adolescents are homosexual or bisexual in terms of attraction or orientation, even if they don't identify as gay (Reis and Saewyc, 1999). It is likely that some students who will come out as adults have not yet come to terms with being gay, or are reluctant to report their sexual orientation on a survey administered in school.

GLBT YOUTH OF COLOR

GLBT youth from racial and ethnic minority groups face unique challenges that reflect the multidimensionality of their life situations. Nearly half (48 percent) of GLBT youth of color report verbal harassment based on both their sexual orientation and their race or ethnicity (Kosciw and Cullen, 2001). GLBT youth of color often face homophobia from their respective racial or ethnic group, racism from within a predominantly white GLBT community, and a combination of the two from society at large (Hunter and Mallon, 2000). Feeling as if one has no community to identify with or that one must choose between various aspects of one's identity can be especially burdensome to GLBT youth of color (Dube and Savin-Williams, 1999).

Research on the influences of race and ethnicity on sexual identity development is limited (Kumashiro, 2001). Traditional sexual identity development models, such as Cass's (1979) stage identity model, are based primarily on cohorts of white gay men. Many researchers question the applicability of these models to identity development among GLBT youth of color and women (Dube and Savin-Williams, 1999). The dearth of research on GLBT youth of color has been documented by Ryan (2002) for the National Youth Advocacy Coalition. Ryan (2002) found that in the past 30 years of the 166 academic articles or chapters published on GLBT youth, only 9 articles and 2 book chapters focused on gay, lesbian, or bisexual youth of color. None of the articles focused specifically on transgender youth of color. The report calls for studies on how various ethnic groups socially regulate sexual culture and behavior; how youth of color perceive gender in relation to sexual identity; and the process of sexual and ethnic identity development in GLBT youth of color.

Sexuality holds different meanings within each cultural and ethnic group, and identity is formed, in part, by these meanings. Values and beliefs regarding sexuality, stereotypes about gender and sex roles, expectations of childbearing, religious values and beliefs, degree of acculturation or assimilation into mainstream society, and the importance of family and ethnic communities in providing acceptance and support can disproportionately impact GLBT youth of color (Ryan and Futterman, 2001). For example, the supportive and tight-knit family structures that can be found among Asian and Pacific Islander (API) American, African-American, and Latino communities can make the coming-out process more difficult for some GLBT youth (Greene, 1997). As Trinity Ordona, a cofounder of Asian/Pacific Islander PFLAG (Parents, Families and Friends of Lesbians and Gays) in San Francisco, notes,

> The families are the core of the culture. When a gay Asian comes out and gets kicked out of the family, it's like being severed from the heart. But if you get the family on your side they will stand and protect you. (Varney, 2001, p. 91)

GLBT youth of color often experience racism in white-dominated GLBT communities and organizations (Leck, 2000). Furthermore, support networks such as gay-straight alliances (GSAs) historically have disproportionately helped suburban and middle-class GLBT youth, who tend to be white. Increasingly, GSAs are coming into existence in urban schools with higher proportions of students of color. Work continues to be done to ensure that the diversity of the student body is fully reflected in the membership and the leadership of these clubs. Initiatives to make schools safer for GLBT students and to integrate GLBT issues into the curriculum also must incorporate an understanding of how GLBT youth of color's experiences differ from those of white GLBT students (Kumashiro, 2001).

EDUCATION POLICY ISSUES AFFECTING GLBT STUDENTS

GLBT youth are self-identifying and coming out at earlier ages, are actively supporting one another and advocating for themselves, and are organizing to increase the safety, support, and visibility of GLBT students in schools. Still, public policy has not always kept up with these advances. Teens often come out in schools where administrators and teachers cannot guarantee their safety against verbal and physical attack from other students. Many find that they are not at all represented in school curricula.

Antigay harassment and violence is epidemic in the nation's schools. From elementary school through high school, *gay* is the epithet of choice to denote something bad, undesirable, or just different. Although all students can become a target of harassment for their perceived homosexuality or gender nonconformity, the nation's GLBT students and the children of GLBT parents often suffer the worst abuse (Perrotti and Westheimer, 2001).

Such abuse can have devastating effects on the children targeted, including higher rates of suicidal ideation and attempted suicide, higher truancy and dropout rates, substance abuse, and running away from home. In a 1999 Massachusetts study, almost 49 percent of lesbian, gay, and bisexual students said they had considered suicide during the previous year (Massachusetts Department of Education, 2000).

Sometimes even teachers make statements that create a hostile environment and appear to legitimize harassment and violence against GLBT students. For example, one teacher told his class, after attending a health fair at which people with AIDS spoke, "All gays and lesbians will die of AIDS" (Reis, 1999, p. 26). In another instance, when a student asked about gay issues or AIDS in class, the teacher turned to two students widely thought to be gay and said, "Why don't we ask them? They seem to be the experts."

There are a number of effective policy interventions that government officials can enact to improve school climate and safety. While there are ethical reasons for making the nation's schools safer for gay students, there are also legal reasons: federal law and the U.S. Constitution mandate equal access to education. For example, Title IX of the Educational Amendment Acts of 1972 prohibits severe and pervasive sexual harassment (one guise that antigay harassment can take) and gender-based harassment on failure to conform to masculine and feminine stereotypes or norms. Also, the equal protection clause of the Fourteenth Amendment of the U.S. Constitution guarantees equal protection under the law to all students; one day this may be interpreted by the courts to protect students of a minority sexual orientation or gender identity. Schools that fail to provide a safe environment to GLBT students are also vulnerable to lawsuits that can incur financial liabilities. Jamie Nabozny, for example, was awarded $800,000 because teachers and administrators in his Wisconsin high school didn't take action to stop the daily harassment and violence he experienced (D'Augelli, 2002; Lambda Legal Defense, 1996).

ANTI-GLBT HARASSMENT AND VIOLENCE IN THE NATION'S SCHOOLS

Almost 85 percent of GLBT youth surveyed in the 2001 National School Climate Survey reported hearing homophobic remarks often or frequently from their school peers (Kosciw and Cullen, 2001). More than 80 percent of GLBT youth surveyed reported verbal harassment during the past twelve months because of their sexual orientation; 40 percent said this harassment happened often or frequently. One in five GLBT students reported physical assault over the past year because of their sexual orientation, while 10 percent reported being assaulted because of their gender identity or gender nonconformity. Nearly 70 percent of students reported feeling unsafe in school because of their sexual orientation.

The 1999 Massachusetts Youth Risk Behavior Survey, conducted by the state Department of Education, found that lesbian, gay, and bisexual youth were

- three times more likely than their heterosexual peers to have been assaulted or involved in at least one physical fight in school;
- three times more likely to have been threatened or injured with a weapon at school; and
- four times as likely as their heterosexual peers to skip school because they felt unsafe (Massachusetts Department of Education, 2000).

A study in Des Moines public high schools found that the average high school student hears an antigay comment every seven minutes; teachers intervened only 3 percent of the time (Carter, 1997).

Unchecked, antigay harassment can escalate to violence, including rape. Of 111 incidents of antigay harassment and violence reported to the Safe Schools Coalition of Washington State, 92 targeted students. These included eight separate gang-rape incidents in which eleven children were raped, two of them sixth-graders (Reis, 1999).

Many victims of physical assault fear their parents' homophobic reaction (Reis, 1999). As a result, they don't report such incidents. Furthermore, adult teachers and school staff are often silent or blame the victim. This was the case in about one in four of the cases witnessed by adults reported to the Washington State Safe Schools Coalition (Reis, 1999).

Impact of Antigay Harassment on GLBT and Questioning Youth and the Children of GLBT Parents

Much of the research on GLBT youth has focused on the harmful impact of antigay harassment and paints a predominantly negative picture of school life for GLBT students in the United States. According to this body of research, youth who witness and are the victims of this treatment are at higher risk for suicidal ideation, substance abuse, eating disorders, teen pregnancy, sexually transmitted infections, and other health risks. The 1997 Wisconsin Youth Risk Behavior Survey found that youth harassed because someone thought they were gay were four times as likely as other youth to have made a serious enough suicide attempt within the past twelve months to be treated by medical professionals (Reis and Saewyc, 1999). These youth were also twice as likely to report having sniffed inhalants, three times as likely to have been pregnant or gotten someone pregnant, and four times as likely to have vomited or taken laxatives to lose weight within the past thirty days.

For those who stay in schools where they've been harassed or assaulted, most have a harder time paying attention in class and don't talk as much in class, thus avoiding the attention of potential tormenters (Reis, 1999). Truancy and dropout rates also are higher for gay, lesbian, and bisexual students. The 1991 National American Indian Adolescent Health Survey found that 28 percent of gay Native American youth, compared to 17 percent of their heterosexual peers, had run away from home within the past year (U.S. Department of Health and Human Services, 1991, as cited in Reis, 1999).

Antigay Harassment in Elementary Schools

Although most policy interventions targeting antigay harassment and violence are done in high schools and, to a lesser extent, middle schools, one study found harassment of kids as early as first grade (Reis, 1999). One first-grader, riding home with his father, asked: "Do you know what a 'faggot' is?" His father responded: "Why do you ask?" The child replied, "[Name] called me one at recess." In another reported case, a second-grader was taunted in class and on the playground with "Get away, gay boy!" and "Don't let gay boy touch you!" The boy was unsure why they were saying this about him, what he had done "wrong," or why no one would play with him at recess. Consequently, he was more reserved and less interactive in class, and often preferred to stay home.

While these two incidents evoked a fairly supportive reaction from teachers and school administrators, another situation in which a third-grader was called "faggot," "gay boy," and "joto" (Spanish for "queer") was minimized by the school principal. Even though the mother witnessed the "joto" remark, the principal considered it "hearsay," telling her: "He'll have to live with it." He also refused to call the parents of the harasser, asserting, "Kids of this age don't know what this means" and that a meeting with both students and both sets of parents "wouldn't resolve anything" and would be "totally inappropriate and unnecessary." When she attempted to go over the principal's head, school district administrators never returned the mother's calls. Her son did not want to arrive at school before classes started out of fear of being attacked in the schoolyard. At the end of the school year, she moved him to another school.

CHILDREN OF GLBT PARENTS IN SCHOOLS

In addition to GLBT identified students in schools, the children of GLBT parents also face isolation, harassment, discrimination, and resultant health and educational risks. Their experiences may be both similar and different from those of GLBT identified youth.

Estimates of the number of children of GLBT parents range widely. Some estimates indicate that between 6 and 14 million children have at least one gay or lesbian parent. More conservative estimates find that between 1 and 9 million children ages eighteen and under are being raised by a gay or lesbian parent (Johnson and O'Connor, 2002;

Patterson, 1992; Schulenburg, 1985; Stacey and Biblarz, 2001). According to the 2000 U.S. Census, roughly one of every three lesbian or bisexual female couple households (34 percent) had children under the age of 18 living in the home, as did 22 percent of partnered gay/bisexual men (Black et al., 2000; U.S. Census Bureau, 2003). Similarly, one in five black GLBT people surveyed in the Black Pride Survey 2000 reported being biological parents and 2.2 percent reported being adoptive or foster parents (Battle et al., 2002). Another study found that one in four black lesbians lived with a child for whom she had child-rearing responsibilities, and 2 percent of black gay men reported children in the household (Mays et al., 1998).

The vast majority of children's advocacy organizations, including the American Academy of Pediatrics, the National Association of Social Workers, and the American Psychological Association, recognize that most gay and lesbian parents are good parents, and that children can and do thrive in gay and lesbian headed families (Ferrero, Freker, and Foster, 2002; Perrin and the Committee on Psychosocial Aspects of Child and Family Health, 2002). Patterson (1995) reports "not a single study has found children of gay or lesbian parents to be disadvantaged in any significant respect relative to children of heterosexual parents."

Children of lesbian and gay parents also experience harassment:

> In one school, a sixth-grader was labeled a "fag" by classmates who discovered that he had lesbian parents. Other children would point pencils at his behind and make sexual innuendoes, while teachers who witnessed this harassment failed to intervene. The harassment spiraled out of control, culminating in physical violence. He was thrown against his locker and kicked in the head by a boy wearing cleats. Moments later, he yelled at one of his attackers, and he was later punished for using inappropriate language. His mothers, with the help of a lawyer, quickly had their son transferred to another school. (Perrotti and Westheimer, 2001, p. 108)

Fontaine's 1998 study of school counselors and perceptions of their gay and lesbian students found that many targeted for harassment were those whose parents were gay or lesbian. Children of GLBT parents hear messages from society, their school-age peers, and often school personnel that their families are, at best, nontraditional. Heterocentrism is pervasive in society and tolerated, if not magnified, in public schools (Sears, 1994). These heterocentric assumptions in most early childhood education programs leave most teachers ill equipped to address the needs of these youth (Kissen, 1999; Rubin, 1995).

STRENGTH AND RESILIENCY OF GLBT STUDENTS

Much attention is paid to the victimization of GLBT adolescents and the resultant health risks. Although this is significant in establishing the need for nondiscrimination policies, gay-straight alliances, and staff training, the fact is that most GLBT youth are happy, healthy, and successful (Savin-Williams, 2001a).

Many GLBT youth are thriving in their school environments and are proud of who they are and their accomplishments (Lipkin, 1994). With strengths, talents, and skills at their disposal, these youth are able to develop positive and productive coping strategies, tapping into existing support networks or creating their own (Munoz-Plaza, Quinn, and Rounds, 2002). GLBT youth also often lead efforts to promote policy intervention to make schools safer for themselves and their peers. In Massachusetts, hundreds of GLBT youth successfully lobbied the legislature to pass a gay student rights law banning sexual orientation discrimination in the state's public schools. In California, similar youth-led action and lobbying occurred every year from 1995 to 1999, culminating in more than 700 youth descending on Sacramento in March 1999 to lobby for legislation prohibiting discrimination based on sexual orientation.

Many GLBT students are one another's role models and sources of support (Bochenek and Brown, 2001; Gilliam, 2002; Ginsberg, 1999). Lobbying efforts, such as those in Massachusetts and California, GSAs, and other extracurricular and peer-education student groups, and events such as the student-initiated National Day of Silence, profoundly affect GLBT youth and school climate. GLBT youth gain a sense that they can make a difference and contribute positively to their communities (Lee, 2002).

Although the data regarding GLBT youth suicide are distressing, one study of 11,940 adolescents points out that the majority of the sexual minority youth who were surveyed (85 percent of males and 72 percent of females) reported no suicidality (Russell and Joyner,

2001). In another study of 221 gay, lesbian, and bisexual youth, Proctor and Groze (1994) found that the youth who had not considered or attempted suicide "possessed internal and external qualities that enabled them to cope well in the face of discrimination, loneliness, and isolation" (p. 509).

The strength, resiliency, and self-advocacy of GLBT youth are the subjects of a growing field of inquiry. Researchers, educators, policy analysts, advocates, and GLBT youth leaders are contributing to this body of knowledge. Work is under way to identify the positive impact of interventions, policies, and the innovations that students and school staff are implementing across the country. How can the "internal and external qualities" that Proctor and Groze (1994) discuss be recognized and replicated? What are the innovations that are successful in helping GLBT student leaders advocate for themselves and their peers? In what ways can the data detailing higher rates of suicidal ideation and substance abuse be reevaluated to improve the support and services available to GLBT and questioning youth? There is much to learn.

CONCLUSION

Youth are coming out earlier as gay, lesbian, bisexual, or transgender, but many school administrators and teachers are not keeping up with this cultural change. GLBT youth and children of gay parents are often vulnerable to harassment, violence, and even rape or murder. In schools across the United States, GLBT and supportive straight youth are organizing to make schools safer, more affirming places where GLBT students can develop socially in ways parallel to their heterosexual peers. In future research, we will examine policy interventions aimed at ending anti-GLBT harassment and violence, as well as recent policy innovations that may complicate these efforts.

REFERENCES

Battle, J., Cohen, C., Warren, D., Fergerson, G., and Audam, S. (2002). *Say it loud I'm black and I'm proud: Black pride survey 2000.* New York: National Gay and Lesbian Task Force Policy Institute.

Black, D., Gates, G., Sanders, S., and Taylor, L. (2000). Demographics of the gay and lesbian population in the United States: Evidence from available systematic data sources. *Demography, 37*(2), 139-154.

Bochenek, M. and Brown, A. (2001). *Hatred in the hallways: Discrimination and violence against lesbian, gay, bisexual and transgender students in U.S. public schools.* New York: Human Rights Watch. Available online at <http://www.hrw.org/reports/2001/uslgbt/toc.htm>.

Carter, K. (1997). Gay slurs abound. *Des Moines Register,* March 7, p. 1.

Cass, V.C. (1979). Homosexual identity formation: A theoretical model. *Journal of Homosexuality, 4,* 219-235.

D'Augelli, A. (2002). Fear and loathing in high school. *Penn State Op Ed.* August 22. Available online at <http://www.psu.edu/ur/oped/daugelli.html>.

Dube, E. and Savin-Williams, R. (1999). Sexual identity development among ethnic sexual-minority male youth. *Developmental Psychology, 35*(6), 1389-1398.

Ferrero, E., Freker, J., and Foster, T. (2002). *Too high a price: The case against restricting gay parenting.* New York: ACLU Lesbian and Gay Rights Project. Available online at <http://www.lethimstay.com/pdfs/gayadoptionbook.pdf>.

Fontaine, J. (1998). Evidencing a need: School counselors' experiences with gay and lesbian students. *Professional School Counseling, 1*(3), 8-14.

Gilliam, J. (2002). Respecting the rights of GLBTQ youth, a responsibility of youth-serving professionals. *Transitions* (Advocates for Youth Newsletter), *14*(4), 1-2, 17.

Ginsberg, R. (1999). In the triangle/out of the circle: Gay and lesbian students facing the heterosexual paradigm. *The Educational Forum, 64,* 46-56.

Goodenow, C. (1997). *Massachusetts youth risk behavior survey.* Boston: Massachusetts Department of Education.

Greene, B. (1997). Ethnic minority lesbians and gay men. In B. Greene (Ed.), *Ethnic and cultural diversity among lesbians and gay men* (pp. 216-239). Thousand Oaks, CA: Sage Publications.

Human Rights Watch (2001). *Hatred in the hallways: Violence and discrimination against lesbian, gay, bisexual, and transgender students in U.S. schools.* New York: Human Rights Watch.

Hunter, J. and Mallon, G. (2000). Lesbian, gay, and bisexual adolescent development. In B. Greene and G. Croom (Eds.), *Education research and practice in lesbian, gay, bisexual, and transgendered psychology* (pp. 226-243). Thousand Oaks, CA: Sage.

Johnson, S. and O'Connor, E. (2002). *The gay baby boom.* New York: New York University Press.

Kissen, R. (1999). Children of the future age: Lesbian and gay parents talk about school. In W. Letts and J. Sears (Eds.), *Queering elementary education: Advancing the dialogue about sexualities and schooling* (pp. 165-175). Lanham, MD: Rowman & Littlefield.

Kosciw, J. and Cullen, M. (2001). *The 2001 National School Climate Survey: The school related experiences of our nation's lesbian, gay, bisexual and transgender youth.* New York: Gay, Lesbian and Straight Education Network.

Kumashiro, K. (Ed.) (2001). *Troubling intersections of race and sexuality: Queer students of color and anti-oppressive education.* Lanham, MD: Rowman & Littlefield.

Lambda Legal Defense and Education Fund (1996). Case: *Nabozny v. Podlesny.* 92 F.3rd 446 (7th Cir. 1996). Available online at <http://www.lambdalegal.org/cgi-bin/iowa/cases/record?record=54>.

Leck, G. (2000). Heterosexual or homosexual? Reconsidering binary narratives on sexual identities in urban schools. *Education and Urban Society, 32*(3), 324-348.

Lee, C. (2002). The impact of belonging to a high school gay/straight alliance. *High School Journal, 85*(3), 13-26.

Lipkin, A. (1994). The case for a gay and lesbian curriculum. *The High School Journal, 77*(1/2), 95-107.

Massachusetts Department of Education (2000). *Massachusetts high school students and sexual orientation results of the 1999 Youth Risk Behavior Survey.* Boston: Author. Available online at <http://www.doe.mass.edu/hssss/yrbs99/glb_rslts.html>.

Mays, V., Chatters, L., Cochran, S., and Mackness, J. (1998). African American families in diversity: Gay men and lesbians as participants in family networks. *Journal of Comparative Family Studies, 29*(1), 73-87.

Mortimer, J. (1987). *Youth development study.* Minneapolis: University of Minnesota.

Munoz-Plaza, C., Quinn, S., and Rounds, K. (2002). Lesbian, gay, bisexual and transgender students: Perceived social support in the high school environment. *High School Journal, 85*(4), 52-63.

Patterson, C. (1992). Children of lesbian and gay parents. *Child Development, 63*(5), 1025-1042.

Patterson, C. (1995). *Lesbian and gay parenting.* Washington, DC: American Psychological Association. Available online at <http://www.apa.org/pi/parent.html>.

Perrin, E. and the Committee on Psychosocial Aspects of Child and Family Health (2002). Technical report: Co-parent or second-parent adoption by same-sex parents. *Pediatrics, 109*(2), 341-344.

Perrotti, J. and Westheimer, K. (2001). *When the drama club is not enough: Lessons from the safe schools program for gay and lesbian students.* Boston, MA: Beacon Press.

Proctor, C. and Groze, V. (1994). Risk factors for suicide among gay, lesbian, and bisexual youths. *Social Work, 39*(5), 504-513.

Reis, B. (1999). *They don't even know me! Understanding anti-gay harassment and violence in schools.* Seattle, WA: Safe Schools Coalition.

Reis, B. and Saewyc, E. (1999). *Eighty-three thousand youth: Selected findings of eight population-based studies as they pertain to anti-gay harassment and the safety and well-being of sexual minority students.* Seattle, WA: Safe Schools Coalition.

Rubin, S. (1995). Children who grow up with gay or lesbian parents: How are today's schools meeting this "invisible" group's needs? Unpublished thesis. Madison: University of Wisconsin.

Russell, S. and Joyner, K. (2001). Adolescent sexual orientation and suicide risk: Evidence from a national study. *American Journal of Public Health, 91*(8), 1276-1281.

Ryan, C. (2002). *A review of the professional literature and research needs for LGBT youth of color.* New York: National Youth Advocacy Coalition.

Ryan, C. and Futterman, D. (1998). *Lesbian & gay youth: Care and counseling.* New York: Columbia University Press.

Ryan, C. and Futterman, D. (2001). Social and developmental challenges for lesbian, gay and bisexual youth. *SIECUS Report, 29*(4), 4-18.

Savin-Williams, R. (2001a). A critique of research on sexual-minority youths. *Journal of Adolescence, 24,* 5-13.

Savin-Williams, R. (2001b). Suicide attempts among sexual-minority youths: Population and measurement issues. *Journal of Counseling and Clinical Psychology, 89*(6), 983-991.

Schulenburg, J. (1985). *Gay parenting.* New York: Anchor.

Sears, J. (1994). Challenges for educators: Lesbian, gay, and bisexual families. *The High School Journal, 77*(1/2), 138-154.

Seattle Public Schools (1996). *1995 teen health risk survey.* Seattle, WA: Author.

Stacey, J. and Biblarz, T. (2001). (How) does the sexual orientation of the parents matter? *American Sociological Review, 66*(2), 159-184.

U.S. Census Bureau (2003). *Married-couple and unmarried-partner households: 2000.* February. Washington, DC: Author.

U.S. Department of Human Services (1991). *National American Indian Adolescent Health Survey.* Washington, DC: Author.

Varney, J. (2001). Undressing the normal: Community efforts for queer Asian and Asian American youth. In K. Kumashiro (Ed.), *Troubling intersections of race and sexuality* (pp. 87-103). Lanham, MD: Rowman & Littlefield.

Vermont Department of Health, Division of Alcohol and Drug Abuse Programs (1997). *1997 Vermont youth risk behavior survey.* Montpelier: Author.

Chapter 11

The Research Terrain:
A Brief Overview
of the Historical Framework
for LGBTQ Studies in Education

Laura A. Szalacha

The lead article of the January 2002 issue of *Educational Leadership* suggested five strategies for schools to welcome children from sexual minority families. The journal for *Equity and Excellence in Education* has finalized a special issue focusing on LGBTQ issues in schools. *The Journal of Adolescence* (2001) and the *High School Journal* (1993-1994) have already featured such special issues. Each of these reflects the positive changes in school climates for LGBTQ (lesbian, gay, bisexual, transgender, queer) students, teachers, faculty, and staff, as well as the vast growth and development in the research and scholarship regarding both LGBTQ educational issues and queer theory itself in the past two decades.

SCHOOL CLIMATE

Every teacher knows that a positive and safe school climate is imperative for productive teaching and learning (Tirozzi and Uro, 1997). Students need to feel attached to school as a supportive community that recognizes their individuality and cares about and promotes their success (Bidwell, 1987; Bryk and Driscoll, 1988; Coalition for Essential Schools, 1985; Coleman, 1987; Lightfoot, 1978; Lipsitz, 1984; Young, 1990). Educators recognize that in order to provide a warm and supportive school climate, school administration and support services must be especially sensitive to the needs of students who have responsibilities or problems outside of school (Fraser and Fisher, 1982a,b; Hill, Foster, and Gendler, 1990). Similarly, sexual minority youth experience unique stresses that the school system must also recognize and address (Hunter and Schaecher, 1987, 1995).

Consequently, many educators have taken steps to meet the needs of sexual minority youth and to address homophobia in schools. Fifteen years ago, Sears (1987) asserted that this is due to three general trends: (1) educators acknowledging that all identifiable groups of students need support that is unique to their situation; (2) the increasing numbers of youth declaring their homosexuality while in secondary school; and (3) the victimization of lesbians and gays both in schools and in society at large. In the new millennium, educators are coming to believe that they have a social responsibility to provide an environment that supports the ability of all students—including lesbians, bisexuals, gays, and transgendered persons—to learn and, at the same time, is free from physical and psychological abuse.

Reflective of these trends in the United States, national organizations have declared their support for LGBTQ students' education. The American Psychological Association, joined by the National Association of School Psychologists and the American School Health Association, have called for secure educational atmospheres in which lesbian, gay, and bisexual youths "may obtain an education free of discrimination, harassment, violence, and abuse, and which promotes an understanding and acceptance of self" (American Psychological Association, 1991, p. 9). In 1993, the National Middle School Association adopted a resolution to meet the needs of all young adolescents, including those of sexual minority youth.

It was a decade ago that the National Education Association (NEA) formally recognized that homosexual students experienced great "hostility and neglect" in school environments (1991). The organization's *Training Handbook for Educators* (NEA, 1991) identified the right of every student to "have access to accurate information about themselves, free of negative judgment, and delivered by trained adults who not only inform them, but affirm them" (p. 40). More recently, the NEA has provided an agenda for schools calling for (1) the accurate portrayal of the roles and contributions of gay, lesbian, and bisexual people throughout history, with an acknowledgment of their sexual orientation; (2) the acceptance of diversity in sexual orientation and the awareness of sexual stereotyping whenever sexuality and/or tolerance of diversity are taught; and (3) the elimination of sexual orientation name-calling and jokes in the classroom (NEA, 1995, p. 1). To this end, the NEA offers its members sensitivity workshops, classroom materials, and speakers regarding the needs of gay and lesbian students, crisis intervention, violence prevention strategies, and appropriate responses to expressions of homophobia.

There have been successful metropolitan efforts (e.g., Hetrick-Martin Institute in New York; Project 10 in Los Angeles; and the University of Minnesota Youth and AIDS Project in St. Paul), and individual school initiatives (e.g., Project 10 East in Cambridge, MA). In January 2000, the Buffalo (NY) Board of Education voted to prohibit discrimination on the basis of sexual orientation and to adopt a broad safe school policy that includes teaching respect for diversity.

Wisconsin, the first state with legislation of its kind, mandates that every public school district adopt and disseminate a policy prohibiting bias, stereotyping, and harassment of gay/lesbian/bisexual individuals. In addition, in 1999, Governor Gray Davis signed into law AB 537, the California Student Safety and Violence Prevention Act of 2000. Massachusetts, however, is unique in directly addressing the safety of sexual minority students in its schools from a central board of education. The "Massachusetts Model" (Lipkin, 1999), Safe Schools Program for Gay and Lesbian Students, is the only statewide mandated program of its kind in the United States—although Rhode Island and Oregon have recently been following this model.

Moreover, scores of Web sites and texts are available to assist in the development of gay-straight alliances at the university and secondary school levels, organizations such as the gay/lesbian parent teacher association and SIGNS: School Survival Guide for LGBT Youth and Their Allies, and the ongoing efforts of the local, regional and national offices of the Gay, Lesbian and Straight Education Network (GLSEN).

LGBTQ EDUCATIONAL RESEARCH AND SCHOLARSHIP

Prior to the 1970s in the United States, LGBTQ research and scholarship were dominated by psychological studies of disorder.

More recently, going beyond the documentation of the victimization and suicidal aspects of some LGBTQ students' lives (Hershberger and D'Augelli, 1995; Savin-Williams, 1994), there are calls for more attention to the positive aspects of normative LGBTQ development (Savin-Williams, 2001).

There have been major strides in broadening the scope of research in terms of educational arenas, educational theory, curriculum, and pedagogy. Although the first queer educational research with student populations was conducted only with university students, the scope of current research has expanded to include students at the middle school and secondary levels in the United States (Bailey and Phariss, 1996; Elia, 1994; Friend, 1993, 1998; Uribe and Harbeck, 1992). Researchers now examine ways to influence both the acknowledged curricula in schools (Colleary, 1999; King and Schneider, 1999; Lipkin, 1999), and the "hidden curriculum of sexuality" from preschool through college (Sears, 1999). We now analyze the experiences of LGBTQ educators (Glasgow and Murphy, 1999; Mittler and Blumenthal, 1994) and the intersections of race, class, gender, and sexual orientation of our students (Kumashiro, 1999; Pallotta-Chiaroli, 1999).

There has also been a worldwide emergence of thinking and theorizing by teachers and scholars regarding LGBTQ issues in education in Europe, India, Canada, South Africa, Mexico, and Australia. *Challenging Lesbian and Gay Inequities in Education* (Epstein and Johnson, 1994), for example, examines sexualities and schooling in Great Britain. *Lesbian and Gay Studies and the Teaching of English: Positions, Pedagogies, and Cultural Politics* (Spurlin, 2000) presents the writings of an international group of teachers regarding LGBTQ issues as they relate to teaching and learning of English and composition from elementary through university levels. Essayists, theorizing lesbian, gay, and transgender positions in the classroom, offer pedagogical strategies for teaching lesbian and gay studies as well as examine the broader social and political contexts that shape classroom discourse and practices. A key example is Tatiana de la Tierra's (2000) discussion of the academic and political concerns of consciously addressing lesbian and gay subjects in the pedagogical discourses and approaches used to teach English composition. De la Tierra argues that, by virtue of her identities as a Latina and a fully bilingual and bicultural lesbian, she must be socially responsible: "Acknowledging and working with factors already in the classroom creates an opportunity for it to become a site for social transformation because students are then able to problematize their own positions" (p. 171). As a person of multiple, intersecting positionalities, de la Tierra theorizes about homophobia within other vectors of domination and integrates queer and other differences into the teaching of composition.

There are empirical studies at the first, second, and third level institutions in the European educational systems as well. Buston and Hart (2001), for example, examined heterosexism and homophobia in secondary schools in Scotland. Through a multimethod evaluative study of SHARE (Sexual Health and Relationships–Safe, Happy and Responsible, a two-year, twenty-lesson teacher-led sex education program), they determined that homophobia among male students was very common. These researchers also found that some of the lessons contained explicit homophobia and that others contained implicit homophobia (noted as the "heterosexist presumption"). Nevertheless, in lessons homosexuality was normalized alongside heterosexuality (what the researchers labeled "good practice") and teachers who were concerned about the disadvantages that lesbian and gay young people had to face in the program. Buston and Hart concluded that the key is to develop strategies and communicate them to teachers, "stressing the unacceptability of homophobic comments and behavior in the context of equal opportunities and anti-discriminatory school policies" (p. 108).

O'Carroll and Szalacha (2000) examined the teaching about sexuality and sexual orientation with the introduction of the Relationships and Sexuality Education programme (RSE) in Ireland. Following Ireland's abolition of all previous laws criminalizing homosexual activity and their replacement by a new gender-neutral law with a common age of consent of seventeen for all persons, the RSE was the first attempt by the Irish government to launch a sex education program in its schools. There was strong resistance to the implementation of the RSE, considered by the conservative National Party to be "pornographic and putting children at risk" (O'Carroll and Szalacha, 2000, p. 30). The slow progress of the RSE throughout the country was also complicated by the program planners' initial focus on primary school teachers and boards (as opposed to secondary level schools) and by the right of each school to deliver the program, voluntarily, in line with its own ethos. O'Carroll and Szalacha concluded that this work continues, however, through collaborative partners (administrators, teachers, school boards, and parents) at all levels of policy formation and school implementation.

Elsewhere, Khayatt (1992) examined the experiences of lesbian Canadian teachers. In response to the requests for information from secondary and tertiary Australian students doing assignments or postgraduates beginning research projects on LGBTQ issues, the Gay and Lesbian Welfare Association (GLWA) in Brisbane, Australia, convened a research symposium. Queer in the 21st Century: Perspectives on Assimilation and Integration brought together those actively engaged in local LGBTQ research (Argus and Cox, 1999).

The rapid trajectory of LGBTQ research has progressed to such a level that, although the earliest studies were often conducted with small convenience samples or only clinical populations (often consisting of anecdotal studies), current standards require methodological rigor (e.g., in sampling) and analytic sophistication. In fact, Sears (2002) found in his preliminary review of the LGBTQ educational research conducted during the past 15 years, 75 percent of the more than 400 studies were quantitative. The primary methodology has been survey research (59 percent) with only 7 percent quasiexperimental. Half of the studies were conducted in higher education and 29 percent at the secondary level; only a handful of studies were conducted with early childhood or middle school students. The research has taken place predominantly in the United States (89 percent) with a disproportionate number of Euro-American subjects (93.7 percent). Sexual identity, coming out, and then suicide were the predominant areas of research focus, with studies of the educational environment ranking sixth.

Our present cache of scholarship contains purely quantitative studies, such as Dempsey, Hillier, and Harrison's (2001) study of gendered subjectivity homosexuality of same-sex-attracted Australian youth and wholly qualitative studies, such as Flower and Buston's (2001) retrospective interviews of working-class gay men from a small town in the north of England about gay identity development. There, too, are secondary analyses of large, nationally representative data sets, notably Russell, Seif, and Truong's (2001) examination of school outcomes of sexual minority youth analyzing the data from the National Longitudinal Survey of Adolescent Health. Finally, mixed-methods studies that include both large-scale surveys and interviews/focus groups, such as Szalacha's recent evaluation of the Massachusetts Safe Schools Program for Gay and Lesbian Youth (Szalacha, 2003).

Finally, a striking characteristic of LGBTQ research in education, both in the United States and abroad, is its strong interdisciplinary foundation covering a wide range of intellectual bases: literature, history, religion, psychology, sociology, philosophy, anthropology, medicine, law, fine arts, and others (e.g., Fuss, 1991; Goodenow, Netherland, and Szalacha, 2002; Herek and Berrill, 1992; Rothblum and Brehony, 1993; Sedgwick, 1985; Stein, 1990).

QUEER THEORIES

In 1991, Teresa de Laurentis coined the term *queer theory* for "theorizing lesbian and gay sexualities." Queer theory has developed into a discipline. Investigating the historical and contemporary experiences of LGBTQ persons, academic programs grant certificates or concentrations (e.g., The University of Iowa, Brandeis University, Duke University, University of Wisconsin–Milwaukee), academic minors (e.g., San Francisco State University, Stanford University, Berkeley, Cornell University, George Mason University, Concordia University College [Canada], and majors (Wesleyan University, University of Chicago, Barnard College-Columbia University, Brown University, Hobart and William Smith Colleges). There are also research centers such as the Center for Lesbian and Gay Studies (CLAGS) at the City University of New York.

Whether this movement from marginality to the center will ultimately best serve LGBTQ educational concerns has yet to be established. Mainstream educators and activists chafe at what they view as queer theorists' overly academic approach devoid of practical knowledge. Meanwhile, radical critics of education and curriculum (e.g., Pinar, 1998), echoing the words of Audre Lorde (1984), have cautioned, "the master's tools will never dismantle the master's house." As a primary agent in the socialization of children, educational institutions, as a whole, tend to reify the present hegemonic ideologies—including an essentialist view of human sexuality.

The *Journal of Gay & Lesbian Issues in Education* embraces this tension between theory and practice, educational scholarship, and policy as we extend the efforts of the past two decades. We are building on this expansion with a call for submissions with a clear emphasis on the implications of results to educational policy and practice. For those researchers who have faced the challenges of finding an appropriate venue for publishing their LGBTQ focused educational research, this journal offers an exciting opportunity.

REFERENCES

American Psychological Association (1991). American Psychological Association statements on lesbian and gay issues. Committee on Lesbian and Gay Concerns. Available online at <www.apa.org/pi/statemen.html>.

Argus, J. and Cox, S. (1999). *Queer in the 21st century: Perspectives on assimilation and integration.* Brisbane, Australia: Gay and Lesbian Welfare Association.

Bailey, N. and Phariss, T. (1996). Breaking through the wall of silence: Gay, lesbian and bisexual issues for middle level educators. *Middle School Journal, 27*(3), 38-46.

Bidwell, C. E. (1987). Moral education and school organization. In M. T. Hallinan (Ed.), *The social organization of schools* (pp. 178-209). New York: Plenum.

Bryk, A. and Driscoll, M. W. (1988). *The high school as community: Contextual influences and consequences for students and teachers.* Madison: University of Wisconsin–Madison, National Center on Effective Secondary Schools.

Buston, K. and Hart, G. (2001) Heterosexism and homophobia in Scottish school sex education: Exploring the nature of the problem. *Journal of Adolescence, 24*(1), 95-109.

Coalition for Essential Schools (1985). *Common principles.* Providence, RI: Coalition for Essential Schools, Brown University.

Coleman, J. S. (1987). Families and schools. *Educational Researcher, 16*, 32-38.

Colleary, K. P. (1999). How teachers understand gay and lesbian content in the elementary social studies curriculum. In W. J. Letts IV and J. T. Sears (Eds.), *Queering elementary education* (pp. 151-161). Lanham, MD: Rowan and Littlefield.

de la Tierra, T. (2000). Coming out and creating queer awareness in the classroom. In W. J. Spurlin (Ed.), *Lesbian and gay studies and the teaching of English: Positions, pedagogies, and cultural politics* (pp. 168-190). Urbana, IL: Council of Teachers of English.

de Laurentis, T. (1991). Queer theory: Lesbian and gay sexualities. *Differences: A Journal of Feminist Cultural Studies, 3*(2), i-iv.

Dempsey, D., Hillier, L., and Harrison, L. (2001). Gendered (s)explorations among same-sex attracted young people in Australia. *Journal of Adolescence, 24*(1), 67-82.

Elia, J. P. (1994). Homophobia in the high school: A problem in need of a resolution. *High School Journal, 77*(1), 177-185.

Epstein, D. and Johnson, R. (1994). On the straight and narrow: The heterosexual presumption, homophobias and schools. In D. Epstein (Ed.), *Challenging lesbian and gay inequalities in education* (pp. 195-207). Philadelphia, PA: Open University Press.

Flower, P. and Buston, K. (2001) "I was terrified of being different": Exploring gay men's accounts of growing-up in a heterosexist society. *Journal of Adolescence, 24*(1), 51-65.

Fraser, B. J. and Fisher, D. L. (1982a). Effects of classroom psychosocial environment on student learning. *British Journal of Educational Psychology, 52*(3), 374-377.

Fraser, B. J. and Fisher, D. L. (1982b). Predicting students' outcomes from their perceptions of classroom psychosocial environments. *American Educational Research Journal, 4*, 498-519.

Friend, R. (1993). Choices not closets: Heterosexism and homophobia in schools. In M. Fine and L. Weis (Eds.), *Beyond silenced voices: Class, race, and gender in United States schools* (pp. 209-236). Albany: State University of New York Press.

Friend, R. (1998). Heterosexism, homophobia, and the culture of schooling. In S. Books (Ed.), *Invisible children in the society and the schools* (pp. 137-166). London: Lawrence Erlbaum.

Fuss, D. (Ed.) (1991). *Inside/out: Lesbian theories, gay theories.* New York: Routledge.

Glasgow, K. and Murphy, S. (1999). Success stories of a fat, biracial/black, Jewish lesbian assistant principal. In W. Letts IV and J. Sears (Eds.), *Queering elementary education* (pp. 217-224). Lanham, MD: Roman and Littlefield.

Goodenow, C., Netherland, J., and Szalacha, L. (2002). AIDS-related risk among adolescent males who have sex with males, female, or both: Evidence from a statewide survey. *American Journal of Public Health, 92*, 203-210.

Herek, G. and Berrill, K. (Eds.) (1992). *Hate crimes: Confronting violence against lesbians and gay men.* Thousand Oaks, CA: Sage.

Hershberger, S. and D'Augelli, A. R. (1995). The impact of victimization on the mental health and suicidality of lesbian, gay, and bisexual youths. *Developmental Psychology, 37*(1), 65-74.

Hill, P. T., Foster, G. E., and Gendler, T. (1990, August). *High schools with character* (R-3944-RC). Santa Clara, CA: RAND. Available online at <www.crpe.org/Publications/HSwcharacter/HSwtoc.html>.

Hunter, J. and Schaecher, R. (1987). Stresses on lesbian and gay adolescents in schools. *Social Work in Education, 9*(3), 180-189.

Hunter, J. and Schaecher, R. (1995). Gay and lesbian adolescents. In R. L. Edwards (Ed.), *Encyclopedia of social work,* Volume 7, Nineteenth edition (pp. 1055-1059). New York: National Association of Social Workers.

Khayatt, M. (1992). *Lesbian teachers: An invisible presence.* Albany: State University of New York Press.

King, J. R. and Schneider, J. J. (1999). Locating a place for gay and lesbian themes in elementary reading, writing, and talking. In W. J. Letts IV and J. T. Sears (Eds.), *Queering elementary education: Advancing the dialogue about sexualities and schooling* (pp. 125-136). Lanham, MD: Rowan and Littlefield.

Kumashiro, K. (1999). Reading queer Asian American masculinities and sexualities in elementary school. In W. Letts IV and J. Sears (Eds.), *Queering elementary education* (pp. 61-70). Lanham, MD: Roman and Littlefield.

Lightfoot, S. L. (1978). *Worlds apart: Relationships between families and schools.* New York: Basic Books.

Lipkin, A. (1999). *Understanding homosexuality, changing schools.* Boulder, CO: Westview.

Lipsitz, J. (1984). *Successful schools for young adolescents.* New Brunswick, NJ: Transaction.

Lorde, A. (1984). The master's tools will never dismantle the master's house. *Sister outsider* (pp. 110-113). Freedom, CA: Crossing Press.

Mittler, M. and Blumenthal, A. (1994). On being a change agent: Teacher as text, homophobia as context. In L. Garber (Ed.), *Tilting the tower* (pp. 3-10). New York: Routledge.

National Education Association (1991). *Training handbook for educators.* Washington, DC: National Education Association.

National Education Association (1995). *Understanding gay, lesbian, and bisexual students through diversity: Action sheet.* Washington, DC: NEA Human and Civil Rights.

O'Carroll, I. B. and Szalacha, L. A. (2000). *A queer quandary: The challenge of the inclusion of sexual orientation.* Dublin, Ireland: LEA/LOT.

Pallotta-Chiaroli, M. (1999). "My moving days": A child's negotiation of multiple lifeworlds in relation to gender, ethnicity and sexuality. In W. Letts IV and J. Sears (Eds.), *Queering elementary education* (pp. 71-82). Lanham, MD: Roman and Littlefield.

Pinar, W. (Ed.) (1998). *Queer theory in education.* Mahwah, NJ: Lawrence Erlbaum.

Rothblum, E. and Brehony, K. (Eds.) (1993). *Boston marriages: Romantic but asexual relationships among contemporary lesbians.* Amherst: University of Massachusetts.

Russell, S., Seif, H., and Truong, N. (2001). School outcomes of sexual minority youth in the United States: Evidence from a national study. *Journal of Adolescence, 24*(1), 111-127.

Savin-Williams, R. C. (1994). Verbal and physical abuse as stressors in the lives of lesbian, gay male and bisexual youths: Associations with school problems, running away, substance abuse, prostitution and suicide. *Journal of Consulting and Clinical Psychology, 62*(2), 261-269.

Savin-Williams, R. C. (2001). A critique of research on sexual minority youth. *Journal of Adolescence, 24*(1), 5-13.

Sears, J. T. (1987). Peering into the well of loneliness: The responsibility of educators to gay and lesbian youth. In A. Molnar (Ed.), *Social issues and education: Challenge and responsibility* (pp. 79-100). Alexandria, VA: Association for Supervision and Curriculum Development.

Sears, J. T. (1999). Teaching queerly: Some elementary propositions. In W. Letts IV and J. Sears (Eds.), *Queering elementary education* (pp. 3-14). Lanham, MD: Roman and Littlefield.

Sears, J. T. (2002). Fifteen years later: The draft summary report on the state of the field of lesbian, gay, bisexual and transgender issues in K-16 and Professional Education, A research review (1987-2001). Paper presented at the Annual Meeting of the American Educational Research Association, Seattle, WA, April.

Sedgwick, E. K. (1985). *Between men: English literature and male homosocial desire.* New York: Columbia University.

Spurlin, W. J. (2000). *Lesbian and gay studies and the teaching of English: Positions, pedagogies, and cultural politics.* Urbana, IL: Council of Teachers of English.

Stein, E. (Ed.) (1990). *Forms of desire: Sexual orientation and the social constructionist controversy.* New York: Garland.

Szalacha, L. A. (2003). Safer sexual diversity climates: Lessons learned from an evaluation of the Massachusetts' Safe Schools Program for gay and lesbian students. *American Journal of Education, 110*(1), 58-88.

Tirozzi, G. and Uro, G. (1997). Education reform in the United States: National policy in support of local efforts for school improvement. *American Psychologist, 52,* 241-255.

Uribe, V. and Harbeck, K. M. (1992). Addressing the needs of gay, lesbian, and bisexual youth. In K. M. Harbeck (Ed.), *Coming out of the classroom closet: Gay and lesbian students, teachers and curricula* (pp. 9-28). Binghamton, NY: Harrington Park Press.

Young, T. W. (1990). *Public alternative education: Options and choice for today's schools.* New York: Teachers College Press.

Chapter 12

Bullying and Homophobia in Canadian Schools: The Politics of Policies, Programs, and Educational Leadership

Gerald Walton

Following the 1999 Columbine massacre, administrators in Canada and the United States were increasingly pressed to take action against school violence by parents' groups, teachers' associations, and education critics. Accordingly, antiviolence policies and programs proliferated north and south of the Canadian-U.S. border. Rhetoric of "safe schools" continues to be central to the mission statements and operating principles of school boards.

For Canadians, a "copycat" shooting—as it was quickly labeled—was especially shocking. In the small farm community of Taber, Alberta (known for its grade-A corn crops), a lone student randomly opened fire on his classmates, leaving one student dead and another injured. This tragedy demonstrated to Canadians that such violence is not limited to the United States, to large schools, or to sprawling urban centers.

As a result of the Taber shooting, administrators could no longer be complacent about the potential for similar incidents in Canadian schools. A generalized fear, fueled by media preoccupation and sensationalism, is now the status quo. Public officials, including school board trustees, increasingly have been held accountable for providing safe spaces. Consequently, some schools, notably in the United States,

The author would like to thank Aaron T. Wilson for friendship, partnership, and continual support of his work and Laurel Walton for helpful editorial assistance.

have become fortresses of learning with the addition of surveillance cameras, metal detectors, and security guards.

Canadian school administrators have not readily adopted such invasive measures. Even if they had, it is unlikely that surveillance could have prevented the most high-profile Canadian case of bullying and student violence. The 1997 beating and murder of fourteen-year-old Reena Virk by her peers actually occurred away from school property. Nevertheless, the Greater Victoria School District (GVSD) has been the subject of much media attention. One year later, the provision of safety for all students was officially enshrined in the GVSD mission statement:

> The Greater Victoria School District is committed to each student's success in learning within a responsive and safe environment. (Greater Victoria School District, 2003)

The British Columbia (BC) government has taken similar actions, ostensibly to bolster safety in schools. The BC Ministry of Education (2001a) has "provided an assortment of materials, resources, and training to assist schools, parents, and communities with strategies for prevention and intervention to keep British Columbia schools safe" (p. 18). Such provisions are accessible through the BC Safe Schools Centre, a tripartite collaboration of the BC Ministries of Education and Attorney General, and the Burnaby School District (BC Safe Schools Centre, 2001). Two Ministry of Education publications, *Focus on Bullying: A Prevention Program for Elementary School Communities* (1998), and *Focus on Harassment and Intimidation: Responding to Bullying in Secondary School Communities* (2001b), have found their way onto the bookshelves of school administrators across the country.

Such literature is not unique to British Columbia. Across North America, discourse abounds about so-called safe schools. Antibullying programs have become common currency in school districts and even beyond. In 2003, the city council of Edmonton, Alberta, backed by the local police and school boards, passed the first controversial bylaw that officially banned bullying of people under the age of eighteen (Teotonio, 2003). It remains uncertain how Edmonton's bullies will be identified, how the bylaw will be enforced, and how its efficacy will be determined. However, approximately one year later, only five charges had been laid, according to a constable in the Edmonton

Police Service (personal communication, 2004). School Resource Officers interpret the statistic as a sign that the bylaw is an effective deterrence against bullying.

Given this brief historical overview, I will explore the conspicuous absence of homophobic bullying from safe schools agendas. Typically not acknowledged by educational administrators, homophobic violence arises from historical, political, and cultural antecedents. An understanding of this would enhance the efficacy of antibullying policies and programs.

BULLYING AS POLITICAL

In 2001, I attended a one-day symposium, Understanding and Preventing Bullying: An International Perspective, at which several notable international academics presented their research. As the title suggests, the overall objectives were to discuss the latest empirical research on bullying and to highlight the efficacy of particular intervention and prevention strategies.

In brief, the symposium offered a range of perspectives that in one way or another attempted to grapple with what bullying is and what to do about it. Delegates agreed that bullying occurs in all schools and in all societies, and that strategies for intervention and prevention are vital for ensuring students' emotional and physical safety. The topic of homophobic bullying, however, was mostly absent.

This oversight was not due to a willful collusion among the presenters or to individual failings of any given presenter. Nevertheless, it was curious. I was left wondering why, even at a conference on bullying, the topic of homophobia was barely addressed. Broadening the focus from the symposium to the context of school systems, however, allows possibilities for looking at systemic marginalization (Carlson, 1997).

Despite educational activists who extol the virtues of the so-called three R approach to grade school education, schools have never been merely about academic learning (Battistich et al., 1999). A host of nonacademic agendas for teaching and learning are part of the school experience whether or not they are officially recognized in the formal curriculum (Apple, 1975; Jackson, 1969; Pinar et al., 1995). Schools function, in part, as agencies that perpetuate class stratifications (Young and Levin, 2002), neoliberal market values (Apple, 1996), dominant gender scripts (Frank, 1996), and heterosexuality (Epstein and Johnson, 1994).

Within the context of these functions, homophobic bullying is rife with political and social import. In contrast to other forms of aggressive behavior, bullying is typically considered a relation of power of one or more individuals over another with attacks that are repetitive and intended to harm (Olweus, 1993). The power of heterosexuals and heteronormativity, however, has been ignored. Consequently, the important work of addressing bullying in schools in order to develop and administer prevention strategies is, unfortunately, undermined. Meanwhile, lesbian, gay, bisexual, and transgendered (LGBT) students face stigmatization (D'Augelli, 1998), marginalization (Carlson, 1994), social invisibility (O'Conor, 1995), and pervasive accusations of deviance (McLaren, 1995), while discussions in schools about related issues are usually prohibited (Epstein, 1994). Simultaneously, heterosexual identities and relations are normalized.

Straightness is imbued with the status of being "normal" and "natural" not only through gender socialization but through construction of sexual *otherness* as inferior. Heterosexuality in schools is validated through pervasive discourse on teenage other-sex dating; straight sexual mechanics and pregnancy in sex education classes; straight territorialization (such as high school dances and prom nights); and mass media images, textbook representations, and fictional stories exclusively about and featuring heterosexual relationships. Sites of compulsory heterosexuality (Rich, 1993), such as schools, enshrine straightness and marginalize LGBT individuals.

Heterosexual social privilege is being challenged, as in the case of Ontario (then) high school student Marc Hall. In 2002, Marc took his Catholic public school board to court for not allowing him and his boyfriend to attend the high school prom (Smith, 2002). Ultimately, an Ontario Superior Court ruled in his favor.

The privileging of heterosexuality is not only directed at LGBT students such as Marc Hall who are out in their schools but is hidden justification for those who silence such students. The threat of violence for gender and sexual orientation nonconformity is pervasive, though often implicit. These are very negative reactions to *all* students who do not conform to dominant expectations of gender and sexuality—the sissies, dykes, queers, fags, homos, and lezzies—and who challenge, by word, appearance, or deed, the pervasive assumption that straightness is "natural" and "normal." What few consider is that were "natural" and "normal" unproblematic categories, as many assume, then heterosexuality—both private acts and public expressions—would not have to be the compulsory curriculum and bolstered through legal mechanisms that reward heterosexual couplings, deny equal rights to gays and lesbians, and even criminalize homosexuality and particular sexual acts.

During the 1980s, the (then) Toronto Board of Education considered the issue of homophobia in schools after a fatal gay bashing of a school librarian at the hands of five male high school students (Campey et al., 1994). Eventually, the board agreed to promote equity for marginalized students on the basis of racism, sexism, homophobia, classism, and ableism (Toronto District School Board, 2000). The Triangle Program was designed specifically to meet the educational and social needs of LGBT youth (Toronto District School Board, 2001). The program, the only one of its kind in Canada, acts as a "safe space" for students whose educational needs are unmet in conventional school settings where homophobia is pervasive (Solomon, personal communication, December 7, 2001).

However, Triangle functions necessarily as a crisis management program through a strategy of segregation. As beneficial as it might be to the students, the separation of LGBT students from the rest of the Toronto student population does not challenge educators about homophobia in their schools, nor does it require respect for sexual diversity among other students. Had these schools been places where diversity was respected, Triangle students and their (presumably) supportive parents would never have felt compelled—perhaps driven—to this program. As a result, Triangle addresses *acute* cases of student marginalization because of homophobia.

At the Understanding and Preventing Bullying symposium, I listened eagerly for some discussion about homophobia, heterosexism, and LGBT students. None occurred except when I raised the issue during the question-and-answer session. The response, in short, was that homophobia is a pervasive problem in schools. Several people indicated to me afterward that they were glad the issue had been raised.

"SAFETY" FOR SOME, BUT NOT FOR ALL

Merely discussing LGBT issues in schools or including homophobia in antibullying programs compels some people, particularly parents, to metaphorically froth at the mouth. Although some parents are supportive, many express concern that discussions about *homosexuality* might have some undue influence on their children or that educational administrators are undermining what their children are taught at home. Teachers often avoid discussing LGBT issues in the classroom because of such parental concerns or administrative reactions (O'Conor, 1995). Acts of homophobia against students are even perpetrated by a few teachers and administrators (O'Conor, 1995; Uribe and Harbeck, 1992).

Addressing homophobia in antibullying programs and integrating LGBT issues in schools are battles of power and ideology. Groups such as Parents, Families and Friends of Lesbians and Gays (PFLAG), for example, advocate for antihomophobia education, while conservative organizations in BC, such as Focus on the Family Canada (2003) and the Citizens' Research Institute (2003), virulently oppose it. Meanwhile, interested students have formed school-based organizations that promote education on and provide support for LGBT students and allies. In BC, for example, YouthCo AIDS Society (2003) and Gay Youth Services (2003) provide information and resources, and Youthquest (2003) organizes drop-in sites across the province, many of which are located in smaller towns and rural areas. In Toronto, TEACH (Teens Educating and Confronting Homophobia, 2003) and Trans Youth Toronto (2003) provide similar services and resources, as does Rainbow Youth Talk (2003) in Ottawa. Unfortunately, such drop-in sites and Web sites are limited to youth who can access them in safety.

Some teachers have also formed antihomophobia or LGBT-positive organizations. Gay and Lesbian Educators of BC (GALE BC; <www.galebc.org>), for example, advocates full inclusion of LGBT students in all aspects of the school environment, promotes measures to protect the safety of LGBT students, and circulates educational literature on homophobia and heterosexism in schools (Gay and Lesbian Educators of BC, 2000). There are no other comparable organizations in Canada, although EGALE (Equality for Gays and Lesbians Everywhere), Canada's only national LGBT lobby group, is initiating a national education network (James Chamberlain, personal communication, July 17, 2003).

Most parents and educators recognize that strategies to reduce and prevent violence must be implemented to bolster safety in schools, especially in light of recent, sensational, and homicidal school incidents. Typical media representations of school violence (popularly consumed by the public through newspapers, television, magazines, and the Internet) fuel a moral panic among parents in every reading, in every viewing. Similarly, the fear of discussing sexual diversity or addressing homophobia has also fueled a moral panic. The fact that both school violence and homophobia are integrally related is lost on many adults.

Educational policies and accompanying programs typify bullying as a problem of *specific* children who need specific interventions or punishments. There is no focus on systemic problems (e.g., homophobia) that manifest some of these behaviors[1] or on how structural changes in curriculum, policy, or teaching can reduce school violence by fostering respect for sexual diversity. Furthermore, methods employed to augment school safety are limited in scope to confronting acts of *physical* violence through enforcement of zero-tolerance policies (Casella, 2001). Such policies, designed to prevent weapons-related violence, do not consider the cultural and societal antecedents of violence in schools. Neither do these policies or programs consider *psychological* violence. Thus, this focus on physical violence alone, in combination with antibullying initiatives that avoid homophobia, indicates that safety is enhanced for some students and not others, even in school districts that purport to provide "safety for all students." Most school administrators heartily embrace "safety" but avoid the more challenging but pervasive issues of homophobia, heterosexism, and heteronormativity. Generic strategies for increased safety in schools simply do not address forms of homophobic violence and, consequently, leave some of the most vulnerable students unsafe.

Effective strategies to reduce physical violence and increase school safety are unlikely. In this light, promoting school safety and preventing bullying is largely a public relations exercise. The mission statement of the Greater Victoria School District (2003), for example, states clearly that the district is "committed to each student's success in learning within a responsive and safe environment." This is the same district that fourteen-year-old Reena Virk attended high school in before her beating and murder.

The Surrey School Board in BC also claims to be committed to providing "safe and caring learning environments . . . and promoting tolerance and respect for diversity" (Surrey School District, 2004). The board has also consistently banned (from use in classrooms) three picture books for children that feature families with gay or lesbian parents, preferring to privilege the religious considerations of some parents. This position has remained unchanged despite vocal opposition from an ad hoc parents' group and a ruling from the Supreme Court of Canada, although two other picture books featuring same-sex parents were eventually approved (Perelle, 2003).

A CALL FOR LEADERSHIP IN SCHOOLS

It is unrealistic to claim that violence of all forms can be eliminated from schools. Children, like adults, will inevitably fight over property, space, and stature; will form alliances against other students; will malign one another with verbal taunts; and will intimidate one another through physical aggression. In short, even exemplary educational leaders using inclusive antibullying programs will not have schools completely free of violence.

Furthermore, violence is culturally valorized, legitimized, and supported through discourses of nationalism, vengeance, male privilege, religious zeal, and several media venues of entertainment. School-based violence is, therefore, not adequately explained by theories or addressed by programs or policies that emphasize *individual* behaviors arising from discriminatory or hateful attitudes. Homophobia, like racism and sexism, manifests as violence perpetrated by an individual or group but links to larger social realms of politics, public policy, legal structures, and institutional processes.

Creating schools as safe spaces for *all* students seems a bleak prospect in the face of such pervasive, insidious violence. Some students, though, are particularly at risk. For many LGBT students, prejudice, discrimination, and violence are often part of their daily experiences. Educational leaders are complicit through their inaction and through employing ineffectual, punitive zero-tolerance policies or antibullying programs that emphasize behavior modification.

Beyond the limited role of individual accountability, the development of whole-school cultures of nonviolence is essential. Teachers and administrators are key leaders in forming such a culture; few have taken up the challenge. Similarly, teacher education programs in Canadian universities and colleges tend to focus on curriculum and pedagogy while issues concerning equity in education compose a minor portion of undergraduate education programs. Curriculum that addresses homophobia and heterosexism in schools is left to the discretion of the professor.

Educators in Canada have a wealth of resources from which to draw, including their own professional associations. The British Columbia Teachers' Federation (BCTF) (2003) and the Alberta Teachers' Association (ATA) (2003), to name only two, have developed programs for teachers on LGBT issues, especially concerning pedagogical practice and at-risk youth. Gay and Lesbian Educators of BC (2000) and the McCreary Centre Society in BC (2003) likewise provide educators with resources and strategies for reducing homophobia in schools and for supporting LGBT-inclusive classrooms. Morton (2003) focuses on the particular needs of LGBT youth in rural areas of Canada. Addressing homophobia in schools, therefore, is not confounded by a shortage of resources for educators, regardless of geographical location.

Some Canadian educators have shown leadership concerning the development of cultures of safety and inclusion in schools. For example, Peggy Sattler, a trustee for the Thames Valley District School Board in Ontario, stated recently that policies exist to address all forms of harassment, but

> the bigger problem is the climate of homophobia that exists in our school system, and this [reflects] societal attitudes in many ways, but we want to . . . do some education about the values of tolerance and respect for difference among our students so that we can do some work to prevent the use of homophobic language in our schools. (Canadian Broadcasting Corporation, 2003)

Trustees of the Peel and Bluewater District School Boards (both in Ontario) have also demonstrated such leadership. In the face of potential vitriolic opposition, they have supported broad-based approach efforts of individual teachers to curb homophobia in schools, to support

LGBT students, and to foster increased safety for *all* students. The Peel District School Board in Mississauga, Ontario, provides educators with resources (1) on building respectful environments by challenging seven common "isms" (including heterosexism) and (2) on working with principles of social justice (2003).

Trustees must provide educational leadership concerning the problem of homophobia in schools. Educators, too, can (and do) contribute in a number of ways, such as by educating themselves about LGBT issues and by drawing connections to how such issues influence the culture of schools and the school lives of students. Astute educators can use incidents of homophobia as "teachable moments" for education, thereby modeling a pro-LGBT climate in the classroom.

For trustees and administrators who remain resistant to implementing antihomophobia measures in schools, the potential of incurring costly student-led lawsuits, such as that initiated by (former) student Marc Hall, might be a convincing motivator. In fact, for students who have been systematically victimized by homophobia and ignored by their educators, the Canadian court system is proving to be a powerful but costly form of redress. The school districts of Vancouver, Victoria, and Prince George have taken significant measures to overhaul policy and to develop educational programs to bolster safety for students. The Vancouver School Board has developed an anti-harassment policy that includes sexual orientation and monitors safety issues for LGBT students. The Greater Victoria School Board voted in favor of designing and implementing policy and programming on homophobia and heterosexism, including forming an advisory committee on LGBT-friendly classrooms. Similarly, the province of British Columbia recently organized a task force on safe schools, cochaired by an openly gay public servant (MacMullin, 2002). The task force reported that homophobia "figured prominently" in submissions made to the task force (Mayencourt, Locke, and McMahon, 2003, p. 12) but unfortunately did not make specific recommendations for school boards from which homophobia could be addressed.

Designing and administering antibullying programs and policies is socially responsible work. Some students have probably been spared from a measure of peer bullying as a direct result of such programs, even if public relations and politics have been the central motivators. A critical examination of concepts such as "safety" and "bullying"—

words that have become common currency in educational discourse—highlights historical, cultural, social, and political contexts. Keeping such contexts in mind provides a way of addressing questions posed by Lewis (personal communication, September 10, 2001), such as: "Why this? Why here? Why now?" Asking such critical questions and understanding complex problems such as bullying and homophobia are crucial for improved educational administration on "safe schools."

NOTE

1. One of my criticisms of literature on bullying is that it is taken to be antisocial behavior. This is a misconceptualization because bullying affords dominance and social status and is often rewarded and supported by other children. It may not be nice, but it is, nevertheless, very social.

REFERENCES

Alberta Teachers' Association (2003). *Sexual orientation and gender identity* (content developed by Kris Wells). Available online at <www.teachers.ab.ca/diversity/Sexual_ Orientation/Index.htm>.

Apple, M. (1975). The hidden curriculum and the nature of conflict. In W. Pinar (Ed.), *Curriculum theorizing: The reconceptualists* (pp. 95-119). Berkeley, CA: McCutchan.

Apple, M. (1996). *Cultural politics and education.* New York: Teachers College Press.

Battistich, V., Watson, M., Solomon, D., Lewis, C., and Schaps, E. (1999). Beyond the three R's: A broader agenda for school reform. *The Elementary School Journal, 99*(5), 415-432.

BC Ministry of Education (1998). *Focus on bullying: A prevention program for elementary school communities.* Victoria: Special Programs Branch.

BC Ministry of Education (2001a). *Diversity in BC schools: A framework.* Victoria: Special Programs Branch.

BC Ministry of Education (2001b). *Focus on harassment and intimidation: Responding to bullying in secondary school communities.* Victoria: Special Programs Branch.

BC Safe Schools Centre (2001). Available online at <www.safeschools.gov.bc.ca/the_centre.html>.

BC Teachers' Federation (2003). *Issues in education: Stopping homophobia.* Available online at <www.bctf.ca/Social/homophobia/brochure.html>.

Campey, J., McCaskell, T., Miller, J., and Russell, V. (1994). Opening the classroom closet: Dealing with sexual orientation at the Toronto Board of Education. In S. Prentice (Ed.), *Sex in schools: Canadian education and sexual regulation* (pp. 82- 100). Toronto: Our Schools/Our Selves.

Canadian Broadcasting Corporation (2003). Interview by Erika Ritter (host) of Peggy Sattler on the radio program, *Ontario Morning,* April 11.

Carlson, D. (1994). Gayness, multicultural education, and community. *Educational Foundations, 8*(4), 5-25.

Carlson, D. (1997). *Making progress: Education and culture in new times.* New York: Teachers College Press.

Casella, R. (2001). *At zero tolerance: Punishment, prevention, and school violence.* New York: Peter Lang.

Citizens Research Institute (2003). Available online at <www.citizensresearchinst. com/entry.html>.

D'Augelli, A. (1998). Developmental implications of victimization of lesbian, gay, and bisexual youths. In G. Herek (Ed.), *Stigma and sexual orientation: Understanding prejudice against lesbians, gay men, and bisexuals* (pp. 187-210). Thousand Oaks, CA: Sage.

Epstein, D. (1994). Introduction: Lesbian and gay equality in education—problems and possibilities. In D. Epstein (Ed.), *Challenging lesbian and gay inequalities in education* (pp. 1-10). Buckingham, United Kingdom: Open University Press.

Epstein, D. and Johnson, R. (1994). On the straight and the narrow: The heterosexual presumption, homophobias and schools. In D. Epstein (Ed.), *Challenging lesbian and gay inequalities in education* (pp. 197-230). Buckingham, United Kingdom: Open University Press.

Focus on the Family Canada (2003). Available online at <www.fotf.ca>.

Frank, B. (1996). Masculinities and schooling: The making of men. In J. Epp and A. Watkinson (Eds.), *Systemic violence: How schools hurt children* (pp. 113-129). London: Falmer.

Gay and Lesbian Educators of BC (2000). *Challenging homophobia in schools: A K to 12 resource for educators, counselors, and administrators to aid in the support of, and education about lesbian, gay, bisexual, and transgender youth and families.* Vancouver: GALE BC.

Gay Youth Services Available online at <www.lgtbcentrevancouver.com/main. htm>.

Greater Victoria School District (2003). Mission statement and beliefs. Available online at <www.sd61.bc.ca/html/mission.html>.

Jackson, P. (1968). *Life in classrooms.* New York: Holt, Rinehart and Winston.

MacMullin, G. (2002). Task force wants safer schools. *Outlooks Vancouver,* December, p. 6.

Mayencourt, L., Locke, B., and McMahon, W. (2003). Facing our fears, accepting responsibility: Report of the Safe Schools Task Force, bullying, harassment, and intimidation in BC schools. June 11. Available online at <mla.governmentcaucus. bc.ca/media/SSTF%20REPORT%20Final%20-%20June%2011%202003.pdf>.

McCreary Centre Society (2003). Available online at <www.mcs.bc.ca/mcshome. htm>.

McLaren, P. (1995). Moral panic, schooling, and gay identity: Critical pedagogy and the politics of resistance. In G. Unks (Ed.), *The gay teen: Educational practice and theory for lesbian, gay, and bisexual adolescents* (pp. 105-123). New York: Routledge.

Morton, M. (2003). Growing up gay in rural Ontario. *Our Schools/Our Selves, 12*(4), 107-118.

O'Conor, A. (1995). Who gets called queer in school? Lesbian, gay, and bisexual teenagers, homophobia, and high school. In G. Unks (Ed.), *The gay teen: Educational practice and theory for lesbian, gay, and bisexual adolescents* (pp. 95-101). New York: Routledge.

Olweus, D. (1993). *Bullying at school: What we know and what we can do.* Cambridge: Blackwell.

Peel District School Board (2003). Available online at <www.peel.edu.on.ca/facts/ equity.htm>.

Perelle, R. (2003). "Good start" in Surrey: Two gay-friendly books okayed. *Xtra West,* July 10, p. 13.

Pinar, W., Reynolds, W., Slattery, P., and Taubman, P. (1995). *Understanding curriculum: An introduction to the study of historical and contemporary curriculum discourses.* New York: Peter Lang.

Rainbow Youth Talk (2003). Available online at <www.rainbowyouthtalk.com>.

Rich, A. (1993). Compulsory heterosexuality and lesbian existence. In L. Richardson and V. Taylor (Eds.), *Feminist frontiers III* (pp. 158-179). New York: McGraw-Hill.

Smith, G. (2002). Gay teen wins prom fight. *Globe and Mail,* May 11, pp. A1, A10.

Surrey School District (2004). Say no to discrimination. Available online at <www. sd36.bc.ca/general/info%20brochures/Mission%20Statement%20SD36.pdf>.

Teens Educating and Confronting Homophobia (2003). Available online at <www. ppt.on.ca/teach.html>.

Teotonio, I. (2003). Edmonton bullies to face $250 fine: First Canadian city to pass bylaw against bullying. *Toronto Star,* March 12, pp. A4.

Toronto District School Board (2000). *Equity foundation statement and commitments to equity policy implementation.* Toronto: Toronto District School Board.

Toronto District School Board (2001). *Welcome to the Triangle Program.* Available online at <http://schools.tdsb.on.ca/triangle/program.html>.

Trans Youth Toronto (2003). Available online at <www.icomm.ca/the519/ programs/lgbt/transtoronto.html>.

Uribe, V. and Harbeck, K. (1992). Addressing the needs of lesbian, gay, and bisexual youth: The origins of Project 10 and school-based intervention. In K. Harbeck

(Ed.), *Coming out of the classroom closet: Gay and lesbian students, teachers, and curricula* (pp. 9-28). Binghamton, NY: Harrington Park Press.

Young, J. and Levin, B. (2002). *Understanding Canadian schools: An introduction to educational administration,* Third edition. Scarborough, ON: Thomson Nelson.

YouthCo AIDS Society (2003). Available online at <www.youthco.org>.

Youthquest (2003). Available online at <www.youthquest.bc.ca>.

SECTION III:
PROGRAMS AND PRACTICES

Chapter 13

Serving the Needs
of Transgender College Students

Brett Beemyn

The examples are many:

- A college student gets called "fag" and "queer" because he looks effeminate.
- A campus climate assessment survey asks respondents to rate the environment in the classroom for people of "both genders."
- A diversity training session acknowledges the different genders of participants by asking the women and then the men to stand.
- A college admission form asks applicants to check a box marked "M" or "F."
- A transgender student avoids using certain rest rooms on campus because of hostile comments about his gender.
- A student is afraid that he will not be hired in his profession after graduation if faculty members discover that he has transitioned from female to male.
- A transsexual graduate student wonders how she can change her student records to reflect her gender identity and how she will be received by the students she will be teaching.

These incidents occurred in the past year at The Ohio State University where I work as the coordinator of Gay, Lesbian, Bisexual, and Transgender Student Services. But they could have taken place at any college or university, and, I suspect, few schools have not experienced such acts of intolerance and ignorance around issues of gender identity and the inclusion of transgender students.

There is no accurate measure of the number of transgender college students (just as there are no reliable statistics on the number of lesbian, gay, and bisexual students). Direct observation and anecdotal evidence suggest that youth who do not fit stereotypical notions of "female" and "male" are becoming much more visible on North American campuses and a growing number of students are identifying as gender variant or, as many describe themselves, "gender queer."

Yet colleges have been slow to recognize, much less provide support to, transgender people. Although many lesbian, gay, and bisexual student organizations and almost all of the existing campus LGB administrative offices have added a "T" (signifying transgender) to their names in the last decade, this move toward greater inclusiveness has been more symbolic than substantive. Most LGB student leaders and center directors still have little understanding of the experiences of transpeople and continue to engage in trans-exclusive practices. Other administrators and faculty typically are even less educated about transgender issues and only become cognizant of the needs of transgender students when a crisis arises, such as a conflict over a transitioning woman using the women's rest room.

In fairness to unknowing staff and faculty members, there is yet to be any empirical research on the experiences of transgender college students, and almost nothing has been written about transgender issues in higher education (Carter, 2000). With this in mind, I begin by providing a brief history of the discourses and terminologies that have characterized gender-variant individuals and the subsequent movement among transpeople to define themselves and describe their experiences. I then relate these issues to higher education by discussing the narratives by transgender people in Kim Howard and Annie Stevens's (2000) *Out and About on Campus: Personal Accounts by Lesbian, Gay, Bisexual, and Transgendered College Students,* the first work on college students to include the stories of transgender youth. I conclude by offering recommendations for educators seeking to improve the campus climate for transgender people, based on my experiences as an openly trans-identified administrator working in LGBT student services. Because most colleges and universities create a hostile environment for gender-variant students, staff, and faculty, there is much that institutions can and must do to become more welcoming to people of all genders.

A NOTE ON LANGUAGE

Complicating any discussion of transgender issues is the lack of a sufficient vocabulary. Only now are words being developed to describe the diversity of gender identity and expression, especially the experiences of transpeople who do not exclusively identify as female or male (Cromwell, 1999). But it is not simply the absence of terminology that has been problematic; existing language also fails to capture the complexities of gender. Feminist theorists have popularized the idea that "gender" is socially constructed, in contrast to biological "sex," in order to challenge assumed gender roles (Butler, 1990; de Beauvoir, 1953). But as shown by the unnecessary surgeries performed on intersex infants (that is, on babies whose anatomical characteristics do not fit neatly into "female" or "male") to make their bodies conform to a rigid gender category, "sex" is likewise socially and, at times, literally constructed (Koyama, 2001).

Intersex genital mutilation also points to how "sex" is commonly reduced to one aspect of gender, the person's genitalia. This has the effect of reinforcing a kind of biological determinism that ignores other important components of gender and the ways in which people actually experience their gender (Bornstein, 1998). For example, as I will discuss, few transsexual men have genital surgery, but they do not feel that this makes them less of a man (Cromwell, 1999), and a growing number of transsexuals who have surgery continue to see themselves as transsexual, rather than identifying as "female" or "male" (Bornstein, 1994). In order to avoid making "genital gender" the defining aspect of gender, I will only use the term *sex* as a descriptor for individuals when citing commonly used language.

TRANS-SEXOLOGY

As it is commonly used today, *transgender* is an umbrella term for anyone whose self-identification or expression crosses or transgresses established gender categories, including, but not limited to, transsexuals (individuals who identify with a gender different from their biological gender), cross-dressers (the term preferred over *transvestites*), drag kings, and drag queens. Although this understanding of gender variance is contemporary, developing in the early

1990s with the growth of a transgender movement in the United States and parts of Europe (Wilchins, 1997), people who challenge societal notions of "male" and "female" have existed in many different cultures and time periods (Bullough, 1975; Cromwell, 1999; Docter, 1988; Feinberg, 1996).

In the United States, reports of women and men who cross-lived and/or cross-dressed have appeared in newspapers, legal records, and medical journals since the sixteenth century (MacKenzie, 1994). For example, firsthand accounts of white explorers and missionaries demonstrate that "women-men" and "men-women" were widely recognized in traditional Native American cultures (Lang, 1999). The writings of European and U.S. sexologists in the nineteenth century included many case histories of individuals who saw themselves as belonging to the "opposite" gender and/or who lived as members of the "opposite" gender (MacKenzie, 1994).

But conflating gender with sexual practice, the literature categorized these individuals as "sexual inverts" or "homosexuals." Indeed, many sexologists considered transgender behavior to be the sine qua non of homosexuality (Currah and Minter, 2000). The first researcher to publish widely on homosexuality, Karl Heinrich Ulrichs, theorized in the 1860s and 1870s that what he called "Uranism" resulted from an individual having a gendered soul different from his or her biological gender. Basing his theory primarily on himself, Ulrichs believed that Uranians constituted a "third sex" who loved others of the "same" gender as a person of the "opposite" gender—a description that would be seen today as more characteristic of transsexuality than homosexuality. The most influential nineteenth-century sexologist, Richard von Krafft-Ebing, likewise failed to recognize a distinction between homosexuality and cross-gender identity. Whereas Ulrichs argued that the inborn nature of "inverted" gender expression required an end to the legal and social persecution of such individuals, von Krafft-Ebing classified transgenderism as a sexual perversion and a sign of "moral insanity" (Bullough and Bullough, 1993; Hekma, 1994; MacKenzie, 1994).

Not until Magnus Hirschfeld coined the term *transvestite* in *The Transvestites: The Erotic Drive to Cross-Dress* was gender expression separated from sexual behavior (Hirschfeld, 1991). Hirschfeld, a pioneer in the study of sexuality and an openly gay man who cross-dressed, argued that transvestism was an identity unto itself and that transvestites could be male or female and heterosexual, homosexual, bisexual, or asexual. Relying on the case histories of sixteen men and one woman, he provided one of the first accurate descriptions of cross-dressers:

> In the apparel of their own sex they feel confined, bound up, oppressed; they perceive them as something strange, something that does not fit them, does not belong to them; on the other hand, they cannot find enough words to describe the feeling of peace, security and exaltation, happiness and well-being that overcomes them when in the clothing of the other sex. (p. 125)

Hirschfeld, though, failed to distinguish between cross-dressing and transsexualism. In fact, several of the people he studied who felt a strong desire to be a gender different from their birth gender would be considered transsexuals today (Bullough and Bullough, 1993; Hirschfeld, 1991). The term *transsexual* began to enter the medical literature in the late 1940s and early 1950s (MacKenzie, 1994; Meyerowitz, 1998), especially through the work of endocrinologist Harry Benjamin (1953, 1966), who described a continuum of cross-gender behavior ranging from transvestism to transsexualism.

Transsexuality entered public consciousness through the 1952 media sensation over the gender transition of Christine Jorgensen. As the first person from the United States to go public after undergoing a "sex change" operation, Jorgensen became "the most talked-about girl in the world" when the former World War II soldier returned from surgery in Denmark as what newspaper headlines described as a "blonde beauty" (Serlin, 1995). Although Jorgensen was the first widely recognized transsexual, the earliest known case of transformative surgery was performed in 1882 on Herman Karl (born Sophia Hedwig), a female-bodied man (Bullough and Bullough, 1993). By the 1930s, stories of European "sex changes" appeared regularly in U.S. tabloid newspapers and magazines, demonstrating that a transsexual identity "did not depend on the invention of synthetic hormones or the development of sophisticated plastic surgery techniques" (Meyerowitz, 1998, p. 161).

But the publicity given to Jorgensen and the creation of a commercially feasible process for synthesizing hormones and better methods for sex reassignment surgery in the 1950s (Bullough and Bullough, 1998) led to a deluge of requests for medical intervention from other transsexuals. Jorgensen received hundreds of letters from "men and women who also had experienced the deep frustrations of lives lived in sexual twilight" (Jorgensen, 1967, p. 150); Danish officials were so overwhelmed with visa requests from people seeking surgery that they forbade such operations for foreigners (Meyerowitz, 1998). Doctors in the United States, though, did not begin to perform sex reassignment surgery until the mid-1960s because of a lack of training in the procedures and a lack of understanding of transsexuality itself, reflecting the belief among many psychiatrists that transsexuals needed mental, rather than physical, intervention (Califia, 1997). But as psychotherapy was shown to have no impact on an individual's gender identity, it became clear that if "the mind of the transsexual cannot be adjusted to the body, it is logical and justifiable to attempt the opposite, to adjust the body to the mind" (Benjamin, 1966, p. 91).

Some in the psychiatric community, though, still view transsexuality as a mental illness, albeit one whose prescribed treatment is often hormones and surgery. In 1980, the American Psychiatric Association added "transsexualism" to its third edition of the *Diagnostic and Statistical Manual of Mental Disorders* (DSM-III), and has listed "gender identity disorders" in subsequent editions, despite opposition from many transsexuals, who resent having to be diagnosed as sick and deviant in order to gain medical assistance. Lesbian, gay, and bisexual activists succeeded in removing "homosexuality" from the DSM's list of mental disorders in 1973. Transgender people, however, have been clinically studied less than lesbians, gay men, and bisexuals and are not as well organized to demand access to medical intervention without stigmatization. Thus, the mental health profession continues to contribute to the stereotyping of transsexuals (Bullough and Bullough, 1998; Cole and Meyer, 1998).

The predominance of the "gender identity disorder" model, along with the extensive media coverage accorded to Jorgensen, has also led to the popular myth that all transsexuals desire sex reassignment surgery—specifically that all transsexuals are biological men who seek to become women (Meyerowitz, 1998). More male-born individuals may have publicly identified as transsexual and sought medical intervention following the visibility of Jorgensen and other transwomen in the 1950s and 1960s, but today about the same number of genetic women and genetic men approach medical providers about altering their genders (Hubbard, 1998). Although most transsexual

men take hormones and many have chest surgery (radical mastecto-
mies and reconstruction of nipples and areola), few pursue phallo-
plasty (construction of a penis). Some opt not to have genital surgery
because of the tremendous expense (much more costly than vagino-
plasty), health reasons, or what are often considered less than adequate results. But many transmen and a growing number of transwomen do not pursue "bottom surgery" because they recognize that
their genitalia is not what makes them a man or woman. They resist
"a system that dictates that one has to be either a man (with a penis) or
a woman (with a vagina)" (Cromwell, 1999, p. 117; Rubin, 1998).

Many transgender people today are also challenging the traditional
medical model that urges them to assimilate, invent a conventional
gendered past for themselves, and not reveal that they are transsexuals or cross-dressers to anyone, including their partners, except when
necessary. As transsexual activist Kate Bornstein (1994) states,

> We're told we'll be cured if we become members of one gender
> or another. . . . Transsexuals presenting themselves for therapy
> in this culture are channeled through a system which labels them
> as having a disease (transsexuality) for which the therapy is to
> lie, hide, or otherwise remain silent. (p. 62)

Since the mid-1990s, Bornstein and other transpeople have publicly
embraced a transgender identity, rather than viewed themselves as either male or female. They have sought to create their own communities
through support groups, the Internet, conferences, publications, and
other social and political networks (Califia, 1997; Cromwell, 1999). In
doing so, they are shifting the discourse on transgenderism from a personal disorder to a cultural one: the inability of society to move beyond
narrow gender categories.

TRANSGENDER IN COLLEGE

Although little has been written about transgender college students, the literature that does exist, along with the handful of published stories by transgender youth themselves, indicates that more
and more college students are rejecting the gender assigned to them
and openly exploring other gender possibilities (Carter, 2000;
Howard and Stevens, 2000; Lees, 1998). College is often the first op-

portunity many gender-variant students have to question their ascribed gender, especially if they are living away from family and childhood friends for the first time (Lees, 1998). The fact that most students establish various aspects of their identities during their college years (Chickering, 1969; Chickering and Reisser, 1993) also helps create a relatively open environment on many campuses that can make gender exploration easier.

For example, Ian Fried, a cross-dressing student who attended a small Ohio college, remembers that even his conservative school was "a pretty open place. In a sense everyone was 'coming out,' trying to figure out who they were and what they wanted to become" (Fried, 2000, pp. 254-255). Fried continually had to explain why he wore dresses and to worry about the reaction of other students, but "in being comfortable with [him]self, [he] found most people incredibly supportive" (p. 253).

Other transgender students, though, have reported greater difficulties. Johnny Rogers was called both "dyke" and "faggot"—once on the same day—while transitioning from female to male at Iowa State University. The stress of constantly having to deal with hostility or the fear of hostility, in addition to the usual stresses of being a student, caused him to contract mononucleosis at the end of the school year in which he began to transition. After completing a master's degree, Rogers was hired as the university's LGBT Student Services coordinator. But feeling burned out from the challenges of transitioning, which included continually having to educate others and a lack of support from both heterosexual and lesbian and gay colleagues, he took a position outside academia the following year (Rogers, 2000; personal communication, May 2002).

At the University of Texas at Austin, Andrew Gray, an openly gay male cross-dresser, likewise had to cope with a lack of transgender acceptance, even from members of the campus lesbian, gay, and bisexual support group. Although Gray felt more comfortable cross-dressing than passing as nontransgender, he could not do so every day because of the amount of energy and fortitude required. Chronicling his experiences wearing a dress and high heels to class for the first time, he describes the positive and negative responses he received; some of the harshest reactions were from students he thought were friends. Gray returned to his apartment early because he was mentally and physically exhausted (Gray, 2000).

INSTITUTIONAL SUPPORT
FOR TRANSGENDER STUDENTS

The ordeals described by Rogers and Gray demonstrate why many gender-variant students still choose to remain closeted if they can (such as by cross-dressing only in private or passing as female or male) and only disclose their gender identities when necessary (such as during a gender transition). Transgender students who identify as heterosexual are often even more invisible, as they rarely feel included in lesbian, gay, and bisexual student groups—despite the recently added "T" in these groups' names. But, just as lesbians, gay men, and bisexuals shouldn't be forced to hide their sexual identities, transpeople shouldn't have to lie, lead double lives, and deny their gender simply to make others comfortable, avoid possible discrimination, and prevent being verbally or physically attacked.

College administrators and faculty members can improve the campus climate for gender-variant students and foster an environment in which people of all genders can more readily be themselves by supporting openly transgender students and by learning and providing accurate information about gender diversity. Unfortunately, even well-meaning student affairs professionals and multiculturally minded instructors often lack basic knowledge about transgender issues, resulting in policies and practices that continue the marginalization of gender-variant individuals. There is a common belief, for example, that almost all transgender students are lesbian, gay, or bisexual, or are transsexuals planning to undergo sex reassignment surgery. This results in campus programs and services that fail to acknowledge heterosexual transpeople, cross-dressers, and individuals who are content to remain outside the categories "male" and "female." Similarly, policies that segregate students by gender, such as rest-room designations, residence hall assignments, and rules on who can join most sports teams and some student organizations, ignore and stigmatize individuals who transcend binary notions of gender (Carter, 2000).

Carter (2000) offers three primary ways for colleges to address the needs of transgender students: end institutional gender divisions; provide direct support services; and educate the campus community about transgender issues. I would add a fourth: develop administrative policies and practices that are trans-inclusive and change those that discriminate against gender-variant individuals. Specifically, I offer the following recommendations to student affairs administrators seeking to improve the campus climate for transgender students.

Create a Well-Funded Campus LGBT Center with a Full-Time Professional Director and Support Staff

Having a center whose mission is to offer programs and services for transgender students, along with lesbians, gay men, and bisexuals, is the most important step a college can take to improve the climate for gender-variant people. An office would provide a visible, long-term transgender presence on campus and serve as a focal point for education and advocacy related to transgender issues. Students would no longer have to assume the primary burden of educating others and working to end discrimination. Instead, they could focus on developing a transgender and trans-supportive community and, most important, devote more time to their course work. With a well-staffed and well-funded LGBT center, "student organizers will burn out less, be more productive in their organizing activities, and greater continuity for the student groups will be established" (Governor's Commission on Gay and Lesbian Youth, 1993, p. 40).

The number of institutions that have established LGBT centers has grown tremendously over the past decade. Prior to 1990, there were only five professionally staffed campus centers, but since then, more than fifty colleges and universities have established LGBT offices with at least a half-time paid director, and others are in the process of doing so (Beemyn, 2002). However, in my experience, many of these centers offer few programs and services for transgender students because staff members lack knowledge about transgender concerns and are unsure of how to provide support. The directors of LGBT centers must, therefore, take it upon themselves to learn about the needs of transpeople, and the search committees for these positions must hire candidates who have experience working on transgender issues.

Institutions that cannot establish an LGBT center because of political or financial circumstances should appoint a presidential commission or standing committee on LGBT issues in consultation with students, staff, and faculty and designate an official administrative liaison to the campus LGBT community.

Train the Trainers on Transgender Issues

Many schools have a Safe Zone, Safe Space, or Allies program to raise awareness and understanding of the experiences of LGBT people and to create visible allies among staff, faculty, and administrators. But as with LGBT centers, most of these programs include little, if any, trans-specific content, even though transgender issues are invariably much less understood than lesbian or gay concerns. Before trainers begin offering workshops, they need to educate themselves about transgender experiences and make sure that they are presenting both trans-specific and trans-inclusive material. Using "LGBT" when the circumstances being described are not applicable to transgender people is an insult, not inclusion.

Provide Training on Transgender Issues to Student Affairs Administrators and Other Staff Members Who Regularly Interact with Students

Training should seek to raise awareness and knowledge about the experiences of transgender people, discuss the skills necessary to be a good ally, and lead to the development of a list of concrete actions that participants agree to take to improve the environment in their workplace for people of all genders. Workshops should be highly interactive and address the situations likely to be faced in participants' offices. For example, a training involving campus security staff should discuss how they can be sensitive to the needs of transgender students who have been the victims of hate crimes and how they can handle complaints about a "man" in a women's bathroom. Student health center nurses and doctors should be asked to talk about the specific health care needs of students who are cross-dressing or transitioning.

Staff members asked to attend a training session should include but not be limited to senior administrators, counseling center staff, police officers and other public safety officials, health workers, student union personnel, residential advisors and hall directors, campus religious leaders, financial aid and registrar's office workers, and clerical and support staff throughout the campus (Governor's Commission on Gay and Lesbian Youth, 1993).

Develop Policies and Procedures for Addressing Transphobic Violence and Harassment

Hate crimes against individuals perceived as gender variant are rampant in society and often ignored by the media, police, and lawmakers. In the past decade, an average of one person a month has been reported killed because of his or her gender identity or expression (Remembering Our Dead, 2002). Many more murders of transgender people are not covered in the press or investigated as possible antitransgender hate crimes by law enforcement agencies.

Harassment and violence against lesbians, gay men, and bisexuals are also predicated on gender variance. Rarely do homophobic attackers know someone's sexual identity; they target those who fit the stereotypes of gay men as feminine and lesbians as masculine.

Colleges must implement a zero-tolerance policy for harassment and violence against gender-variant people and clearly and visibly outline the consequences of trans-motivated hate crimes and hate incidents. All students, staff, and faculty should be made aware of where they can turn if they have been victimized and be given the option of anonymous reporting. Even if not required to do so by state law, institutions should keep track of hate crimes on campus against individuals because of their gender identity or expression.

Assist with the Creation of a Group for Transgender and Gender-Questioning Students

Many transgender students feel isolated. They know few other trans-identified students, lack role models, and often do not have a sense of belonging anywhere on campus. A support or social group for gender-variant students would enable them to feel part of a community and less alienated from college life, which can lead to a greater sense of self-worth and increase the likelihood that they will remain in school.

At the same time, LGBT student organizations should be encouraged to become more trans-inclusive, beyond just having the word *transgender* in their names and mission statements. To be truly supportive, they should seek to create a welcoming space for heterosexual transgender students, as well as those who identify as lesbian, gay, and bisexual. For example, meetings should be held in a location that is private enough for students to feel comfortable attending cross-dressed or changing their clothes when they arrive. Transpeople should not have to disclose their gender identity to the whole campus just to come to a meeting.

Recognizing that transgender students are often hesitant to become involved in LGBT groups because of concerns about transphobia, the leaders of LGBT organizations should make a point of greeting *all* new members before and after meetings, always use trans-inclusive language, and not make assumptions about the gender and sexual identities of participants. LGBT groups should also sponsor programs on transgender topics regularly and include transgender perspectives in other programs.

Offer Trans-Specific Programming

Speakers, performers, and films on transgender topics should be brought to campus regularly as part of general student programming so that the burden of providing trans-focused activities does not fall solely on transgender students. Transgender speakers and performers who are popular with campus audiences include Leslie Feinberg, Loren Cameron, Kate Bornstein, Jamison Green, and Riki Anne Wilchins. Among the recent documentaries and feature-length films about transgender experiences that have been well received are *Southern Comfort* (2001), *A Boy Named Sue* (2000), *Ma Vie en Rose* (my life in pink) (1997), *Boys Don't Cry* (1999), *The Iron Ladies* (2000), and *Hedwig and the Angry Inch* (2001).

Use Trans-Inclusive Language on School Forms, Printed Materials, and Web Sites

College forms that ask students to indicate whether they are female or male, and brochures and Web sites that use "he/she" ignore the complexities of gender; these signal to transgender students that they do not belong at the institution. Offering more inclusive language would not only be supportive of trans-identified people but also help educate the campus community about gender diversity. For example, when "transgender" was added as a possible response to a question asking the students' gender on a residence life survey at Michigan State University, the issue sparked discussions in the campus newspaper and among residence hall staff and students. According to Michigan State's director of residence life, the opportunity to self-identify as transgender and the reaction it generated have been a "positive, thoughtful experience" (Lees, 1998, p. 40).

Add "Gender Identity" to the College's Nondiscrimination Policies

College nondiscrimination policies include "sex" and sometimes "sexual orientation" as protected categories. Neither necessarily applies to transgender people, who face discrimination based on their gender identity and expression, rather than their biological gender or sexual identity. To alleviate this shortcoming, some colleges, beginning with the University of Iowa in 1996, have added the words *gender identity* to their equal-opportunity statements. Other institutions that have written policies prohibiting discrimination against gender-variant people include American University, Brown University, University of Washington, Rutgers University (whose policy is applicable only to "individuals who have changed sex or are in the process of changing sex"), Knox College, Kalamazoo College, and DePauw College (Transgender Law and Policy Institute, 2002). Changing a college's nondiscrimination policy is not going to bring an immediate halt to harassment and violence against transgender people—any more than having "race" as a protected category for nearly forty years has ended racial oppression. But it does give gender-variant students necessary legal recourse and, like the use of trans-inclusive language by college officials, sends a message to the campus community that people of all genders are worthy of respect.

Establish a Mechanism to Change the Gender Designation on College Records

Students who are transitioning from one gender to another should be able to have their new gender reflected on college documents, including identification cards, transcripts, financial aid, employment forms, and enrollment records. Besides being a matter of fairness and respect, an accurate gender designation in college files is critical to avoid outing transgender students and to help protect them from discrimination when they apply for jobs, seek admission to graduate and professional schools, and at any other time that they must show a college document. An institution should never insist that individuals complete sex reassignment surgery before changing their records, as even transsexual students who desire surgery often cannot afford the procedures and many transmen feel that the surgical outcomes are still inadequate, since techniques have not been developed to produce a "natural-looking," fully functional penis. Moreover, given that some transgender youth may be uncertain about undertaking the long, arduous process of transitioning, "nothing is gained by forcing a student to hasten into surgery simply for the correct bureaucratic designator" (Nakamura, 1998, p. 185).

Create and Publicize the Location of Unisex Rest Rooms and Enable Transpeople to Use the Rest Rooms They Find Appropriate

One of the main areas where transgender people experience discrimination is in use of public rest rooms. The "bathroom issue" is particularly a problem for transsexual women, but "butch lesbians" and other masculine-appearing women are also often harassed in women's rest rooms, despite being biological women (Nakamura, 1998). Nontransgender women should be able to feel safe in this most private of public environments. So, too, should transsexual and other gender-variant women, who have a right to use the rest room appropriate for their gender. An administrator seeking to mediate a rest room conflict needs to balance the desires of both the transgender student and the complainant; however, a transperson should never be denied access to adequate bathroom facilities simply because of someone's transphobia.

A recent court ruling in a school case recognizes that prejudice does not supercede the basic right of a transgender person to use a public bathroom. When a Minneapolis high school teacher complained about a female transsexual librarian using the faculty women's rest room at the school, the administration provided the teacher with access to other bathrooms, including single-occupancy facilities. Unsatisfied with the school's accommodation, the teacher sued, seeking to ban the librarian from all of the women's rest rooms. Both a federal court and the U.S. Court of Appeals upheld the school's policy as a reasonable solution (Gender Advocacy Internet News, 2002).

To avoid potential confrontations and to make campus rest rooms more accessible to transgender individuals, colleges should publicize the location of single-occupancy bathrooms and designate more uni-sex facilities. Ohio University's Office of LGBT Programs, for exam-ple, launched a "LGBT Restroom Project" in 2001 to identify bath-rooms in residence halls and academic and administrative buildings that were not gender-specified and to encourage administrators to make other single-occupancy rest rooms available to people of all genders (Ohio University Office of Lesbian, Gay, Bisexual, and Transgender Programs, 2001).

Have Advocates in Units Where Transgender Students Are More Likely to Encounter Obstacles

Along with rest rooms, other single-gender environments, such as residence-hall floors and locker rooms, are also sites of potential con-flict between transgender and nontransgender students. Having stu-dent affairs administrators who are well versed on transgender issues in units where gender-variant students are likely to encounter preju-dice from their peers can help resolve problems quickly and avoid further stigmatizing the transperson in the situation.

CONCLUSION

Transgender students are attending colleges and universities across North America, whether or not they are visible to faculty, staff, or other students. Implementing these recommendations would begin a process of creating a better campus climate and safer environment for cross-dressers, transsexuals, and other gender-variant people. They would feel more comfortable being out, be less isolated, and, in gen-eral, have a much more positive college experience.

But, it all begins with senior administrators and student affairs pro-fessionals recognizing the tremendous prejudice and discrimination faced by transgender students and making a serious commitment to changing the situation. College officials need to learn the appropriate language to describe transpeople, educate themselves on transgender history, and seek to understand the lives and needs of gender-variant students. Only a concerted, institution-wide effort, supported and spearheaded by a school's central administration, can transform a campus culture of transphobia.

REFERENCES

American Psychiatric Association (1980). *Diagnostic and statistical manual of mental disorders,* Third edition. Washington, DC: Author.

Beemyn, B. (2002). The development and administration of campus LGBT centers and offices. In R. Sanlo, S. Rankin, and B. Schoenberg, (Eds.), *A place of our own: Lesbian, gay, bisexual, transgender services and programs in higher education* (pp. 25-32). Westport, CT: Greenwood Press.

Benjamin, H. (1953). Transvestism and transsexualism. *International Journal of Sexology, 7,* 12-14.

Benjamin, H. (1966). *The transsexual phenomenon.* New York: Julian Press.

Bornstein, K. (1994). *Gender outlaw: On men, women, and the rest of us.* New York: Routledge.

Bornstein, K. (1998). *My gender workbook.* New York: Routledge.

Bullough, B. and Bullough, V. L. (1998). Transsexualism: Historical perspectives, 1952 to present. In D. Denny (Ed.), *Current concepts in transgender identity* (pp. 15-34). New York: Garland Publishing.

Bullough, V. L. (1975). Transsexualism in history. *Archives of Sexual Behavior, 4* (5), 561-571.

Bullough, V. L. and Bullough, B. (1993). *Cross dressing, sex, and gender.* Philadelphia: University of Pennsylvania Press.

Butler, J. (1990). *Gender trouble: Feminism and the subversion of identity.* New York: Routledge.

Califia, P. (1997). *Sex changes: The politics of transgenderism.* San Francisco, CA: Cleis Press.

Carter, K. A. (2000). Transgenderism and college students: Issues of gender identity and its role on our campuses. In V. A. Wall and N. J. Evans, (Eds.), *Toward acceptance: Sexual orientation issues on campus* (pp. 261-282). Lanham, MD: University Press of America.

Chickering, A. W. (1969). *Education and identity.* San Francisco, CA: Jossey-Bass.

Chickering, A. W. and Reisser, L. (1993). *Education and identity,* Second edition. San Francisco, CA: Jossey-Bass.

Cole, C. M. and Meyer, W. J. III (1998). Transgender behavior and the DSM IV. In D. Denny (Ed.), *Current concepts in transgender identity* (pp. 227-236). New York: Garland Publishing.

Cromwell, J. (1999). *Transmen and FTMs: Identities, bodies, genders, and sexualities.* Urbana: University of Illinois Press.

Currah, P. and Minter, S. (2000). *Transgender equality: A handbook for activists and policymakers.* Washington, DC: The Policy Institute of the National Gay and Lesbian Task Force.

de Beauvoir, S. (1953). *The second sex.* H. M. Pashley (Trans.). New York: Knopf.

Docter, R. F. (1988). *Transvestites and transsexuals: Toward a theory of cross-gender behavior.* New York: Plenum Press.

Feinberg, L. (1996). *Transgender warriors: Making history from Joan of Arc to RuPaul.* Boston, MA: Beacon Press.

Fried, I. (2000). It's a long journey, so bring an extra set of clothes. In K. Howard and A. Stevens, (Eds.), *Out and about on campus: Personal accounts by lesbian, gay, bisexual, and transgendered college students* (pp. 244-255). Los Angeles, CA: Alyson.

Gender Advocacy Internet News (2002). Federal appeals court rejects school teacher's lawsuit seeking to keep transgender employee from bathrooms. June 24. Available online at <http://www.gender.org/gain>.

Governor's Commission on Gay and Lesbian Youth (1993). *Making colleges and universities safe for gay and lesbian students: Report and recommendations of the Governor's Commission on Gay and Lesbian Youth.* Boston, MA: Author.

Gray, A. (2000). Wearing the dress. In K. Howard and A. Stevens, (Eds.), *Out and about on campus: Personal accounts by lesbian, gay, bisexual, and transgendered college students* (pp. 83-91). Los Angeles, CA: Alyson.

Hekma, G. (1994). "A female soul in a male body": Sexual inversion as gender inversion in nineteenth-century sexology. In G. Herdt (Ed.), *Third sex, third gender: Beyond sexual dimorphism in culture and history* (pp. 213-239). New York: Zone Books.

Hirschfeld, M. (1991). *Transvestites: An Investigation of the erotic drive to cross dress.* M. A. Lombardi-Nash (Trans.). Buffalo, NY: Prometheus Books. (Original work published in 1910.)

Howard, K. and Stevens, A. (Eds.) (2000). *Out and about on campus: Personal accounts by lesbian, gay, bisexual, and transgendered college students.* Los Angeles, CA: Alyson.

Hubbard, R. (1998). Gender and genitals: Constructs of sex and gender. In D. Denny, (Ed.), *Current concepts in transgender identity* (pp. 45-54). New York: Garland Publishing.

Jorgensen, C. (1967). *Christine Jorgensen: A personal autobiography.* New York: Paul S. Eriksson.

Koyama, E. (2001). The transfeminist manifesto. In E. Koyama, *Transfeminism: A collection* (pp. 3-11). Portland, OR: The Feminist Conspiracy Press.

Lang, S. (1999). Lesbians, men-women and two-spirits: Homosexuality and gender in Native American cultures. In E. Blackwood and S. E. Wieringa, (Eds.), *Female desires: Same-sex relations and transgender practices across cultures* (pp. 91-116). New York: Columbia University Press.

Lees, L. (1998). Transgender students on our campuses. In R. Sanlo (Ed.), *Working with lesbian, gay, bisexual, and transgender college students: A handbook for faculty and administrators* (pp. 37-43). Westport, CT: Greenwood Press.

MacKenzie, G. (1994). *Transgender nation.* Bowling Green, OH: Bowling Green State University Popular Press.

Meyerowitz, J. (1998). Sex changes and the popular press: Historical notes on transsexuality in the United States, 1930-1955. *GLQ: A Journal of Lesbian and Gay Studies, 4*(2), 159-187.

Nakamura, K. (1998). Transitioning on campus: A case studies approach. In R. Sanlo, (Ed.), *Working with lesbian, gay, bisexual, and transgender college students: A handbook for faculty and administrators* (pp. 179-186). Westport, CT: Greenwood Press.

Ohio University Office of Lesbian, Gay, Bisexual, and Transgender Programs (2001). LGBT restroom project. Available online at <http://www.ohiou.edu/glbt/projects.htm>.

Remembering Our Dead (2002). Available online at <http://www.gender.org/remember>.

Rogers, J. (2000). Getting real at ISU: A campus transition. In K. Howard and A. Stevens, (Eds.), *Out and about on campus: Personal accounts by lesbian, gay, bisexual, and transgendered college students* (pp. 12-18). Los Angeles, CA: Alyson.

Rubin, H. (1998). Phenomenology as method in trans studies. *GLQ: A Journal of Lesbian and Gay Studies, 4*(2), 263-281.

Serlin, D. (1995). Christine Jorgensen and the Cold War closet. *Radical History Review, 62,* 136-165.

Transgender Law and Policy Institute (2002). College and university policies. Available online at <http://www.transgenderlaw.org/college>.

Wilchins, R. A. (1997). *Read my lips: Sexual subversion and the end of gender.* Ithaca, NY: Firebrand Books.

Chapter 14

It's Elementary in Appalachia: Helping Prospective Teachers and Their Students Understand Sexuality and Gender

Patti Capel Swartz

In her essay, "Homophobia: Why Bring It Up?" African-American activist and writer Barbara Smith (1999b) notes,

> [C]urriculum that focuses in a positive way upon issues of sexual identity, sexuality, and sexism is still rare . . . [y]et schools are virtual cauldrons of homophobic sentiment, as witnessed by everything from the graffiti in the bathrooms and the put-downs yelled on the playground to the heterosexist bias of most texts and the firing of teachers on no other basis than that they are not heterosexual. (p. 114)

For homophobia in schools to lessen, teacher education programs must interrogate homophobia and the naturalization of heterosexuality. I have found the children's literature classroom to be a place where discussion of these issues can reach prospective elementary teachers. In the classroom, I use a combination of books and Debra Chasnoff's (1995) film *It's Elementary* to discuss homophobia in schools and to provide methods of discussing homophobia, gender, and sexuality in elementary and middle-grade classrooms.

In Chasnoff's film, Marcus, a student at the Manhattan Day School, explains that "homosexuality needs to be talked about [in classes] because heterosexuality is presumed." Yet many education programs do not provide prospective teachers with the knowledge needed for such discussions. Students entering education programs are dedicated to the well-being of children. However, many have not thought about those children whose parents are lesbian, gay, bisexual, transgender, intersex, or queer[1] (l/g/b/t/i/q) or the student who realizes that she or he is "different." Many, too, have not thought through the meaning or impact of homophobia.

CHALLENGING TEACHERS IN APPALACHIA

Most of my children's literature students are white Appalachians living in socioeconomically depressed rural areas and small towns. Many of these prospective teachers are first-generation college students. Some graduated from a K-12 Christian school and for almost all religious belief is important. Most have not begun to think through the ways in which heterosexuality has been normalized in the culture through media messages, social institutions, and cultural expectations. Learning to "read" culture, then, both inside and outside of schools, becomes vitally important to understanding curriculum reform necessary for social and cultural change. *It's Elementary* allows my students to interrogate their prejudices and cultural constructions as well as to think critically about how to introduce such discussions.

My teachers are reluctant to integrate materials about sexuality and gender into the classroom because of fear of name-calling during discussion. However, in their essay "Locating a Place for Gay and Lesbian Themes in Elementary Reading, Writing, and Talking," James R. King and Jennifer Jasinski Schneider (1999) describe how responses to name-calling can open genuine discussion about "why such talk is harmful and inappropriate" (p. 126). Discussing the power of language through name-calling and seeing this as "an intent to demean" (p. 127) is critical since the slurs often bandied about in school hallways by students are seldom addressed by teachers. These discussions reveal how name-calling helps to form and maintain the "mechanisms behind sexist, patriarchal notions of masculinity" (p. 128) requisite to reinscription of heterosexuality as the "norm." My prospective teachers and, eventually, their students, begin to understand the political and social power that language holds, and the ways in which language is often used as a weapon to maintain the status quo. As King and Schneider (1999) write,

Convening talk about language use is reflexive work on language, and that is language arts. The productive move is teacher's reframing of the significance of what is happening as we talk about using labels and the content behind a given label. If the talk is seen as a broader process-level goal of "learning to interrogate labels," or "questioning the propaganda techniques of categorizing people," this is the work of critical thinking. As such, it is firmly within even the most traditional classroom curricula. What we often fail to do is push the discussion to a critical level, where we can examine with our students how labeling works on an essentialized, bigoted reduction of a person to a label, and that picture is inaccurate and incomplete. (p. 128)

How can we help prospective teachers understand bigotry as well as the power of language in maintaining prejudice? How do we help them to understand and challenge heterosexist assumptions? How can we help elementary educators understand the cultural and educational biases that allow heterosexuality to be seen as "normal" and homosexuality, bisexuality, transgenderism, and the intersex or queer individual as "deviant"? How can we help students to understand that heterosexuality has been "naturalized" through cultural constructions and discourse? How can we help our students consider the variety that exists within the human species? How can we help students to understand that sex for reproduction is not necessarily preferable to other sexual behaviors?

When I ask these and other questions I hope my students will more fully understand

- the falsity of binary oppositions; either/or constructions, especially as these are applied to sexuality, i.e., heterosexuality/homosexuality; the ways in which culture inscribes heterosexuality and representative "masculine" and "feminine" behaviors as the norm and the way that it denigrates other constructions of sexuality and/or gender; that constructions of sexuality and gender are not the same, and that there is a wide range of both sexual and gender behaviors; the damage that name-calling and hiding in the closet create; that l/g/b/t/i/q people live full lives, and that they are not simply their sexuality;
- the surety that they will have students who are, or whose parents or other relatives are, sexual minorities.

As Sears (1999) points out in *Queering Elementary Education: Advancing the Dialogue About Sexualities and Schooling,* challenging stereotypical ideas about gender and sexuality requires educators who "model honesty, civility, authenticity, integrity, fairness, and respect" while "creating classrooms that challenge categorical thinking, promote interpersonal intelligence, and foster critical consciousness" (pp. 4-5).

I attempt to do this in my classroom, similar to Thomas W. Price, the principal of Cambridge Friends School in Chasnoff's film. He asserts that community and social values need to be taught at school as well as at home. Not intervening in hate speech, Price says, gives tacit approval for such behavior and such attitudes. If it were wrong, students think, wouldn't the teacher intervene? And what impact does this have on the student who may already realize (or who will "declare later") that she or he is lesbian, gay, bisexual, intersex, transgender, or queer? The perceived need to hide her or his sexuality will persist because "when Johnny Brewster" called names in fourth grade, the teacher didn't step in, reinforcing homophobia.

Sears (1999) argues that "[t]eaching queerly demands we explore taken-for-granted assumptions about diversity, identities, childhood and prejudice" (p. 5). Sexual and gender diversity, he writes, is a "human hallmark" evidenced in wide-ranging gender and sexual combinations. Pedagogically, these "various intersections of biological sex, sexual orientation, gender identity, gender role, sexual behavior, and sexual identity are best visualized as concentric wheels" (p. 6). Conceptually, he argues,

> [S]exual identity is constructed from cultural materials; sexual orientation is conditioned on biological factors. The degree to which this predisposition for (homo)sexual behavior is realized is, in fact, a measure of social coercion and personal resolve. The question, thus, for educators who teach queerly is not what causes homosexuality but what factors contribute to the homophobia and heterosexism that make coping with one's sexual orientation so difficult. (1999, p. 7)

I believe that, as Sears indicates, heterosexism and homophobia are learned through culture and these are "acquired early in life" but "can be reduced through purposive intervention" (pp. 7-8). However, this requires "that we confront our prejudices inculcated through decades of heterosocialization" (p. 8).

CONFRONTING PREJUDICE IN THE CLASSROOM

My children's literature classroom is a starting place for intervention and for confronting those socially constructed prejudices affecting race, class, and ability as well as those constructions of heterosexism and homophobia that diminish the humanity of us all, whether we are homosexual or heterosexual. To that end, I challenge internalized prejudices, heterosexism, and homophobia through readings, class discussion, and writing tasks.

It's Elementary points out that believing that l/g/b/t/i/q people are not present in schools is simply ignoring facts. In the film, Noé Gutierrez speaks in middle and high schools about his own life as a gay man. Gutierrez, who goes into California schools representing a coalition against violence, makes an important point often overlooked in community conversations about gay materials and issues in schools. He says that when a l/g/b/t/i/q person comes into a school to speak, educators, parents, and students think, "Gay people are coming to our schools." However, as Gutierrez states, "I was a child, and I was in school." Neither speakers nor materials that combat homophobia are bringing "something or someone" to the classroom that is not already there. Rather, they provide affirmation for the student who already knows he or she is sexually different and who often suffers the consequences of that difference: name-calling; emotional violence; and, often, physical violence.

The idea that l/g/b/t/i/q people are already in schools, that speakers coming in are not bringing something or someone that is already in school is a simple idea—but one that has *not* occurred to many students in my classes. They are well aware that homophobia and name-calling exists, but have not thought what it means for a student to be without adult protection or role models. Since these prospective teachers have as one of their stated goals to "be there" for *all* of their students, Chasnoff's film challenges them to think about what "being there" means and which students are really included.

My students frequently express surprise that queer identity is often formed at an early age. Despite their awareness of name-calling and homophobia in schools, Gutierrez's comments about queer students allow these Appalachian future teachers for the first time to think about that presence and the meaning of homophobia. In addition to children's books and films, I use a combination of critical articles and personal essays to help them understand these issues. "He Defies You Still: The Memoirs of a Sissy" is effective because the examples Avicolli (1998) provides show the pain of school life when intervention to stop homophobic acts fails. Although students in my classes have witnessed harassment firsthand, they have not allowed themselves to *imagine* the depth of the pain such harassment causes. Avicolli's pain, however, cannot be ignored. After its reading, over and over again prospective teachers recognize that pain, writing about their desire to be there for their students. One reflectively asks,

> Where are the teachers? How could anyone stand by, ignore, or absent themselves when students are tormenting another student? As a teacher, it will be my job to make sure this doesn't happen, and I will. Even young children can understand justice. Having books like *Asha's Mums* available in the classroom and helping children to understand homophobia and name-calling need to be a part of the work in early elementary grades so that school can be a positive experience for all my students.

Social, political, and cultural constructions—creating oppressions of race, class, gender, sexuality, and ability—are closely related. I often use the work of Audre Lorde (1998) and Barbara Smith (1999a). Both have written of the ways in which race and homophobia combine to create oppression, and to deepen and continue internalized oppression. Indeed, homophobia often causes schisms within communities of color. In one of the class readings, *The Horn Book,* Jacqueline Woodson (1995b) writes of her work as a writer who is not merely a black writer or a lesbian writer. Writing "from the very depths of who I am, and in this place there are all of my identities," Woodson feels "compelled always to write about living and how living molds us. I feel compelled to write against stereotypes, hoping people will see that some issues know no color, class, sexuality" (p. 714). She further describes how difference is "pigeonholed" by publishers who bring out African-American books, or books about women only during the months celebrating their history, and that teachers often do not look for books with other than "mainstream" characters until such a student enters their classroom:

> If there is one black child in a classroom, teachers will search high and low for a book about blacks for that child—or only then begin to think about blackness. But what about the white children? What about putting a book that deals with blackness into the hands of a white child? What about giving an admittedly straight reader a book with gay characters, or a child who lives with both parents a book about a single-parent household? (pp. 714-715)

Committed to "writing books that transcend the lines," Woodson turns the world upside down, integrating gay characters, same-sex parenting, intraracial prejudice, and interracial relationships at the same time that she disrupts expected categories of class (p. 715).

Appalachian students do not need to be told the ways in which class or stereotypes about "hillbillies" affect their lives. And because Appalachians are denigrated in the dominant culture because of regional stereotypes, and queer Appalachians in the local culture because of gay bias, many of these students can understand their difficulties and pain. However, in writing of stereotypes and intersections of prejudice, I do not imply that some easy conflation of "isms" is possible, nor is the elision of difference. Rather, as Shane Phelan (1994) describes, coalition forming is possible among groups whose interests in lessening oppressions coincide. This implies an identity politics that goes beyond "simple counting of categories" (p. 155). This demands a pedagogy that recognizes the shifting and fluid nature of the elements of our lives, the varying groups of which we are part or with which we have contact, and the ways in which a desire to increase social justice and lessen oppression allows coalition building and alliances among groups. As Phelan asserts,

> The questions to ask are not whether we share a given position but whether we can commit to the pain of embarrassment and confrontation as we disagree. . . . The question is whether we can *decide* to be allies, and whether we have the strength to follow through on that decision. . . . [In doing so] we are forced to confront one another, to build a ground together. . . . [A]ll of us who share some fragmented parts of a common dream need to

develop the ability to talk to each other . . . refusing the temptation to cloak crucial differences with the cloak of universality while also refusing to harden those differences into identities that cannot be crossed. (pp. 156-159)

In my discussions with prospective teachers, I help them see the similarities in the *results* of oppression. Racist, sexist, classist, and homophobic statements and name-calling, as well as language designed to denigrate students' physical or mental ability, affect targeted students' self-esteem and their adjustment in the school and/or classroom. I also try to help students understand how the intersections of oppression affect many children. Oppressive conditions that affect self-esteem can lead to personal crisis, disassociation from others and from the self, loss of student potential, and, in some cases, suicide.

WRITING THROUGH HOMOPHOBIA

At the Manhattan Day School and at Cambridge Friends School, literature is used to introduce homosexuality and connect it with issues of social justice. Cambridge Friends School teachers, for example, use *Asha's Mums* (Elwin and Lee, 1990) with early elementary students as a way of providing insights, understanding, and empathy, as well as a way of developing a sense of justice. In this book, Asha's class is going on a field trip. Her teacher, however, won't accept her permission slip because it is signed by both of her mothers. She tells Asha that, despite the facts of Asha's life, she can't have two mothers and that the permission slip must be filled out correctly. In *It's Elementary,* students understand Asha's position and the hurt and upset caused by her teacher's actions: students understand just how unjust these actions are.

In my class, we discuss both film and book in terms of exploring the diversity of family structures. Through the use of mapping and clustering activities, I model ways students can provide input about the diversity of family structures, including families with same-sex parents. Because many of these prospective teachers have not examined their internalized homophobia, they often choose to write about *It's Elementary* and *Asha's Mums.*

In a thoughtful essay, one wrote about her religious beliefs. She described her thoughts and feelings as well as the awareness that grew out of discussing the book and viewing the film. Like teacher Thelma Delgado-Josey at Cambridge Friends School, this student recognized that if she is to reach all children, her religious beliefs or personal prejudices must be set aside.

Many young people in Appalachia, just as in other parts of the country, are becoming less homophobic. These students, aware of the effects of homophobia through friends and family, have written about the importance of using such a book as *Asha's Mums* in the classroom. One nontraditional student described her son's response to his gay uncle as one of love not fear—a response she helped to foster and one she plans to use in her future classroom. In another situation, a traditional age student wrote,

> I have a lot of gay and lesbian friends who have never felt right living in this town and for that reason have moved away. Last June I went on the Washington, DC, AIDS ride and a group of almost 1,500 people came together and lived in peace for three [days]. It didn't matter if you were straight, gay, positive, or not. Everyone had an open mind. If we start with our kids young, then maybe they will love.

Asha's Mums and *It's Elementary* allow students to interrogate classroom practice. These resources allow them to examine their preconceptions about sex, sexuality, gender, and the ways in which homophobia is culturally constructed and maintained.

Another excellent book that points out that it is all right to be different, despite the difficulties children face because of gender difference, is Tomi dePaola's (1990) *Oliver Button Is a Sissy*. Oliver, who likes to dance and attends dancing school, is transformed from the object of classmate ridicule to a star, illustrating that people should—and must—be allowed to be who they are to realize their talents. In dePaola's companion film, *Oliver Button Is a Star* (2001), interviews with other adults who were differently gendered children enable prospective teachers to assess the damage of homophobia and heteronormativity.

I ask students to read these two picture books and Leslèa Newman's (1989) *Heather Has Two Mommies* when we view the two films. The combination of books, dePaola's book and film, and *It's Elementary* spark lively discussion and thoughtful journal entries. One discussion was so heated that it continued the next day in a sociology class in which a number of my students were enrolled.

Female students were less threatened by the book than were the males, and were more accepting of Oliver Button's behavior. All students decried his male classmates' behavior. Women students, though, were more critical of the early attitudes the father displayed in the book, wanting Oliver to take up sports. They praised Oliver's mother and Miss Leah (the dancing school teacher) because they accepted Oliver for who he was.

Students also wrote of the discussion in response papers. They talked of the need for such discussions, the lack of opportunity in most classes to examine controversial issues, and their pleasure in being able to examine difficult issues that will affect their lives and work. Despite the loss of one homophobic male student, I consider the discussion a success. We discussed difficult concepts surrounding sexuality and gender, allowing for a richer reading of cultural imperatives and cultural formation during the reading of subsequent books.

As a part of our discussion, we talked of binary oppositions of male and female, homosexuality and heterosexuality, and the "naturalization" of heterosexuality. We examined the complex relationships of physical and cultural components of identity, and the ways in which culture rewards conformity. We explored the cultural expectations that mold children: expectations for playthings, dress, behavior, and, eventually, marriage and children.

Another part of the discussion examined the wide variation in sexuality, from varying chromosomal makeup to cultural overlay (Lorber, 1998; Sears, 1999), and the ways in which sexism relies on homophobia for its very existence. We talked of heterosexuality becoming "transparent" as the expected behavior, defining itself, through comparisons with homophobia, as "normal." In this discussion, we talked of the need for accepting variations in male and female gendered behavior if appreciation and acceptance of difference is to occur in schools and in the culture.

CONNECTING OPPRESSIONS

This conversation led into a discussion of race and binary oppositions attempted through the cultural construction of whiteness as norm: whiteness that defines itself also through what it is not. We examined how race and racism—as legal and social constructions—are constructed in similar ways to homophobia.

Other texts for the class include culturally specific themes: cultural insensitivity in a teacher's renaming of a student in Alma Flor Ada's (1995) *My Name is Maria Isabel;* the history of racism in the United States represented in Mildred Taylor's (1991) *Roll of Thunder, Hear My Cry* or Christopher Paul Curtis' (1995) *The Watsons Go to Birmingham;* attitudes toward Japanese Americans during World War II presented in Graham Salisbury's (1994) *Under the Blood Red Sun;* and Jews under Nazi occupation in Lois Lowry's (1998) *Number the Stars.* In a response paper, one student confessed,

> I had never known about a lot of the things that you told us in class. For instance, the stories about migrant workers and educational inequalities. All of these things are the truth, yet so many don't know or don't care about it. I would have never viewed the film *It's Elementary* which really enlightened me about the importance of educating children instead of letting them draw inconsistent conclusions. I would have missed out on the film about Mildred Taylor and the truth she shows about life in the South, years ago. The struggles of discrimination and racism, horrible schools and overall tough living conditions . . . or the treatment of Indians in this country along with their great tales. These are things that my high school history curriculum just seemed to skip over.

Another student, however, commented that not many prospective educators would write about *Tar Beach* (Ringold, 1996) or books and films about sexuality. Responding to him, I noted that many *did* choose these texts to write about. Nevertheless, his response indicates that not only are stereotypes about Appalachians internalized by "outsiders" but that we have become victims to such stereotypes. Appalachians, because of the prejudices directed toward us, often have a well-developed sense of justice and a sense that others should be left alone. With classroom help seeing how oppressions affect other groups, these teachers-to-be can put themselves in the place of those "others" who are also the victims of prejudice. Although they may not agree personally with queerness in all of its forms, they do not deny the importance of just treatment for *all* students in the classroom.

In discussing literature for older students with my Appalachian college students, I have found that Jacqueline Woodson's books provide interesting critiques of race, prejudice, and sexuality. *From the Notebooks of Melanin Sun* (Woodson, 1995a) and *The House You Pass on the Way* (Woodson, 1999) are particularly useful. Melanin Sun has always been close to his mother. They've enjoyed activities together, until recently. His mother has begun dating someone and, as a result, she has begun spending less and less time with Melanin. He thinks he might like to have a new dad, despite the fact that he misses the time he used to spend with his mother, but then his mother brings her date home—and she is not a man. She is a white woman. Melanin has to come to terms with his prejudices about lesbians and his attitudes toward white people. Melanin hides out, hoping that he won't have to discuss his mother's relationship with any of his friends, but the day comes when he can no longer hide. He learns about friendship, individuality, and the nature and the futility of racism. In time, he accepts and defends his mother's sexual orientation—and he comes to like her partner.

The experiences in *From the Notebooks of Melanin Sun* can also be used well in classroom discussion. Despite cultural stereotypes of Appalachia as homogeneously white, most preservice teachers have had classes with a variety of racial, ethnic, and social groups. Mixed-race marriages, too, are fairly common. Although these prospective educators have not necessarily thought through the ways that race has been constructed socially and legally, and although, in this depressed economic area, prejudices toward affirmative action are strong, my students are willing to discuss class and racial issues. *From the Notebooks of Melanin Sun* permits examination of internalized race prejudice and homophobia in different communities of color. It allows examination of the effects of prejudice on Melanin himself. My students make parallels between Tommi Avicolli's "hiding out" and Melanin's, writing and talking about the ways in which oppressions overlap.

Melanin Sun is valuable for other reasons as well. Like *Asha's Mums,* it demonstrates to preservice educators that not all l/g/b/t/i/q people are white, and, like the characters in *Asha's Mums,* they can and will inhabit their future classrooms. In classroom discussions we again do clustering and mapping, exploring how this book might be used to broaden students' understanding of race, class, sexuality, and gender. The theme of friendship (often discussed in our class) is useful here. We talk of the nature of friendship and how this applies not only to Melanin but also to friends in our lives. We also continue discussions of the "naturalization" of race and how whiteness often becomes invisible—defined by what it is not—through people of color.

In another segment of *It's Elementary*, Terri Strong, a parent at one of the schools where filming took place, deplores the controversy around gay speakers and teaching about gay and lesbian issues. Strong, a woman of color, asks to what extent parent permission should be able to influence school curriculum. Are permission slips going to be sent home and can parents keep their children out of school on days when issues of sexuality and gender are addressed? Not until, she argues, schools also "send permission slips home when talking about Mexican or Dutch or African-American history? 'We're going to be talking about this. Is it okay?'"

Because she discusses permission slips for other components of the curriculum about which prejudice often exists, Strong's position makes clear that homophobia is only one aspect of the social constructions surrounding sexuality and gender, race, class, and ability that still create oppression in the culture and in the schools. Her statement also makes clear that antihomophobic work is necessary. And in this time of erosion of hard-won freedoms, Strong's words could serve as a warning that other controversial materials in the curriculum, such as African-American history, could become even more purged of content than they already are.

Strong's statement illustrates that educational materials designed to reduce prejudice must always be guarded. Until all aspects of our lives and history (including sexuality, heterosexism, and homophobia) are open to classroom discussion, there is a real threat that gains in other areas could be eroded. As Strong realizes, inclusion of materials that allows teachers and students to interrogate heterosexism and homophobia by examining children's conceptions of sexuality and gender, aiding children's realization of the power of language and of the hurt that language can cause through name-calling and hate speech, and engaging children's sense of justice, are vital to school curriculum that will work toward a more just and equitable society, thereby meeting the educational needs of all children.

PARENTS AND FAMILIES

Although my students discuss the necessity to bring multicultural/ multiethnic materials (including books about sexuality and gender) into the classroom, they are also aware of schools' conservativism and the power of parental objections. Consequently, we discuss strategies from interrogation of language that includes hate speech and name-calling to maintaining classroom libraries for students to peruse at school. We also explore the various types of objections that parents might raise. In discussing *Heather Has Two Mommies,* for example, several students said that they would not have a problem from parents if they read the book to students and discussed families. These female students, already employed as aides in Head Start programs, thought that protests would not be geared to family discussion, even to the fact of the two mommies, but rather to the biological explanation of sexual reproduction that is included in the book.

My students also understand that parents and schools—and even they—believe in the sexual "innocence" of children—another reason to object to classroom materials about sexual and gender difference. The knowledge that children have about sexuality, gender, and homophobia is surprising to my preservice educators, even to those with children. The information or misinformation that children in *It's Elementary* display is one of the most shocking elements of the film for many of my students. One, the mother of a nine-year-old daughter, wrote that she had been in denial about the amount of information her daughter and other children know: "I was amazed about how much they already know. I didn't even know about the pink triangle [used in concentration camps in Nazi Germany to designate homosexual prisoners] till a few years ago."

Many of my students feel that elementary-age children are not aware of or concerned about sexuality and gender, and that they know very little about homophobia. *It's Elementary* quickly dispels that idea. Very young children are aware of the words used in name-calling and the children in the film discuss their information. Most of this comes from television and films.

It's Elementary includes clips from the film *Ace Ventura: Pet Detective* (1994). Children are aware of and laugh at the homophobic representations in such films, such as when Ace realizes that he has kissed a man disguised as a woman, and he frantically brushes his teeth and plunges his mouth with a drain plunger. This scene and the discussion of the children help my students realize that children do think about sex and gender, and that homophobic messages from popular culture do affect them.

Books that deal with varying concepts of family are also good to read and reexamine. We talk about how these books can be used in the classroom to discuss constructions of family: Who is it who makes a family and how do families work together? My students understand that children can enter easily into this discussion, for children know a number of different ways that families are constructed.

While Appalachia is seen by other parts of the country as conservative (and it often is), single parenting is common among men and women because of unmarried mothers or divorce. However, family support and family structures remain bulwarks of culture, and prospective teachers are not only aware of the support (or lack of support) that families can provide but also of the ways in which families interact, often with multiple generations in one household. The strength of local families, the cultural imperatives that make family interaction important to the area, and the configuration of families locally allow students wide experience in types of family constellations.

When background reading has been completed about families and personal experience about family constructions has entered discussion, the families of *Asha's Mums* and *Heather Has Two Mommies,* or Johnny Valentine's (1994) *One Dad, Two Dads, Red Dad, Blue Dad,* or even Lucy the cat's family, two gay men, in *Lucy Goes to the Country* (Kennedy, 1998), do not seem unusual. Often, I use mapping and clustering techniques (documented in Chasnoff's film) with students to demonstrate how to initiate and maintain a discussion. For example, in talking about *Asha's Mums* we would start with the word *family* in a circle and add varying constructions of family from the books and from the students' lives in circles joined to other circles and to the center circle.

CHALLENGING DOMINANT THINKING

Some teachers in Chasnoff's film are white, some are people of color; some are out in the classroom as l/g/b/t/i/q people, some are not; some teachers doing antihomophobic work are heterosexual. In an article in *College English,* Mary Elliot (1996) asserts that despite what teachers often would like to suppose, the classroom is not a neutral space: "neutrality . . . is a universal cultural default setting which is almost always presumed to be heterosexual and white; it is not available to those who cannot 'pass' as either or both" (p. 698). As Elliot, who is out in her college classrooms, indicates, the teacher "coming out [in the classroom] challenges dominant thinking and institutional heterosexism [and] provides a model and personal contact for gay, lesbian, and heterosexual students alike, facilitating the unlearning of prejudice" (p. 698).

This challenge to dominant thinking, however, applies to the teacher whether or not lesbian, gay, transgender, bisexual, or heterosexual. The naturalization of heterosexuality must be challenged if no child is to be left behind in the educational system. As Wayne Martino (1999) points out in "'It's Okay to Be Gay': Interrupting Straight Thinking in the English Classroom," teachers can "help students interrogate familiar patterns of thinking that often resort to defining sexual identity in oppositional terms and as a stable category" (p. 137). This interrogation points out difficulties with conceptions of heterosexuality and rigid gender expectations as "natural." It helps students begin to understand the power of language in creating social and political constructions, and the role of cultural messages in monitoring "acceptable" sexual and gender behaviors through negative representations and binary oppositions.

Challenging the naturalization of heterosexuality arises from a number of my classroom readings, films, discussions, and writings. This teaching can create the possibility of moving "beyond positions of mere acceptance and tolerance of the *other* to encourage students to think about what we take for granted as 'normal' and 'natural'" (Martino, 1999, p. 147). This is more than teaching tolerance; it requires moving beyond tolerance that denies that equality is possible or desirable. The use of such books as *Asha's Mums, Oliver Button Is a Sissy,* and *From the Notebooks of Melanin Sun* allow children to begin to understand the humanity of all people, and "what is."

Positing a continuum of sexuality with prospective teachers and working with them to examine ways to bring difference into the classroom is vital to educational and social change. Children can understand and discuss the diversity of choices among gender roles and the performance of those roles that truly allows sex and gender to be seen in ways that are neither stereotypical nor prejudicial.

In discussions, it is also possible to go beyond the usual depiction of homosexuality as being only about sexuality without regard for the complexity of a whole person, to question why hate speech and labels are applied to people, and to point out—as Cora Sangree does in *It's Elementary*—that l/g/b/t/i/q people form communities, hold jobs, go to school, live in families, create families and build friendships, rather than being one-dimensional persons whose lives revolve around sexuality.

HETEROSEXUAL TEACHERS' RESPONSIBILITIES

As teachers point out in Chasnoff's film, it can be easier for heterosexual teachers to work with queer issues than it is for sexual minority teachers. Often, preservice teachers have not thought about anti-homophobic work as a part of *their* work. Chasnoff's film allows them to think about the need for all teachers, queer or other, to work on these issues.

My students discuss the difficulty that queer teachers encounter as a part of the discussion of the film. Because of the new awareness of homophobia and their responsibilities as educators, many of these heterosexual students consider—often for the first time—negative consequences, such as loss of employment, student confidence, or community standing.

Practicing and prospective teachers—even conservative Christians from small towns and rural areas of Appalachia—can understand that prejudice and homophobia are not only the concern of l/g/b/t/i/q people but the business of *all* people in education. When heterosexuals, including social studies teacher Robert Roth in Chasnoff's film, teach about these issues, they are seen by students (too often socialized to believe that only l/g/b/t/i/q people talk about homophobia) as issues for everyone.

As discussed earlier, confrontations and discussion with parents, in schools, or in communities, as undesirable as they can seem, can be educative—particularly for straight allies who have seldom had to personally confront homophobia. Ellen Varella, Peabody School principal, decided to go forward with the photography exhibit Love

Makes a Family (Kaeser, 1999), despite dissent from some parents and members of the community. Varella says that a lesbian mother warned her that Varella, who is a heterosexual woman, might lose her job over this controversy. While stating that she is not a "flag bearer," this principal continued to work with the exhibit because she "felt strongly children in this community needed to be educated around this topic." Chasnoff's film thus provides role models for prospective heterosexual teachers and administrators.

PEDAGOGICAL AND PERSONAL STRUGGLES

Similar to the teachers who discussed Love Makes a Family with students, students in my classes usually realize that talking with children about constructions of family, about name-calling, and homophobia is vital to a wholesome learning environment. This does not mean that I do not have homophobic students or that my student evaluations are always stellar (in fact they are often lower because of homophobia). But aside from one student who continued in the class whom I felt I could not reach, most students in my children's literature sections have written about their prejudices. This particular student came from a strong religious background, often hearing homosexuality condemned from the pulpit. During the course of the semester, Leslèa Newman was lecturing about the censorship history of *Heather Has Two Mommies* at another campus. Because we were reading her book, I arranged to take interested class members to the lecture, which was sponsored by the campus l/g/b/t/i/q group. The president of the group announced other activities for National Coming Out Week before Newman's introduction. This one student was furious because the lecture was a part of coming-out activities. She was sure that our group contained the only heterosexual people in the room, and later she said she felt that she should have been "warned" about the context for the lecture. Not only did she verbalize these sentiments inside and outside of classes, she also wrote about the "betrayal" she felt in response papers and on her student evaluations. Although she wrote a number of response papers about homosexuality, she remained homophobic throughout the class, despite the comments of and discussion with other students who tried to change her attitudes. She was caustic in her evaluations, rating my teaching and the class at the lowest levels. She was undoubtedly the student I most needed to reach, but I was unable to do so.

As an out teacher, I have found it helpful to be open and honest with students, discussing my own internalized prejudices and how I continually work toward awareness and lessening of these. Using my life as a text in the class helps to destabilize rigid gender, class, and sexual roles as well. I am a formerly married white woman academic who has three adopted children and eleven grandchildren. I am also a person who claims a lesbian identity in the classroom, despite problems with such narrow labeling. My life destabilizes rigid categories and hierarchies. It is particularly important in small southern communities for people to realize that l/g/b/t/i/q people are very much like themselves—and may even be their grandmothers or mothers.

My coming out has given many students their first experience of "knowing someone who is homosexual." It also offers evidence to those students who are not out that it is possible to live a full, productive, and happy life—and to be an educator. The damage that occurs when people must stay in the closet is aptly demonstrated in Chasnoff's film by Jeff, the movement coach for first- and second-graders at Cambridge Friends School. Jeff demonstrates the difficulty of playing soccer using only one leg and foot. He likens that difficulty to being afraid to come out, noting the degree of lost energy and potential of the person who feels she or he must stay in the closet.

If students are to become good teachers, they must be reflective, recognizing their internalized prejudices and oppressions internalized through cultural messages. No attitude must remain fixed: We are all subjects learning with each experience, subjects who are growing and changing. In a discussion of Lesbian and Gay Pride Day at Cambridge Friends School included in *It's Elementary,* one of the teachers noted that what she is "trying to have people do is to realize that people just are. . . . The way that it is, is how it is. [Gender and sexuality are] never neat and tidy and without any conflict because we don't live all by ourselves."

In my life story, such either/or categories, like those that regulate gender and sexuality, are fictions. This is important to convey to students. Discussing binary oppositions, writer/activist Kate Bornstein (1994) writes: "The choice between two of something is not a choice at all, but rather the opportunity to subscribe to the value system which holds the two presented choices as mutually exclusive alternatives" (p. 101). We need to help children (and their teachers) see that containment in those categories is not possible and, in fact, is damaging to all. We must realize, as Audre Lorde (1998) writes, that each of us has "a piece of the oppressor . . . planted deep within" (p. 539); a piece of the oppressor that we must recognize and change.

It's Elementary is a beginning—as is my classroom work with a new generation of elementary teachers to provide the pedagogical tools to help children question false binaries. Granted, the books used in my classroom to interrogate sexuality, gender, and, especially, homophobia are often essentialist oriented. However, critical pedagogical use can extend discussion to the complex interrelationship between physical attributes and culturally constructed attitudes about sexuality and gender, and investigation of the cultural constructions of homophobia and heterosexism that are vital to preserve teachers understanding of student difference.

It's Elementary is not a picture of all schools. Many of the schools, administrators, and teachers portrayed in the film are in communities where there is a greater acceptance of difference than in Appalachia. However, this extraordinarily important film allows future teachers to see the possibilities for educational change—and to discuss how this might be brought about in their small towns and rural communities. Unfortunately, the film is not used widely enough and teacher educators often advise students to stay away from controversial issues. Use of such films as *It's Elementary* is a way to begin that change, to move toward fully educating *all* children. As educator and philosopher Glorianne Leck (1999) observes, "It is unacceptable to deprive children of credible information about their sexuality, about human and social diversity, and about the abuse of power within families, within schools, and within religious group relationships" (p. 259). Yet the unacceptable has been accepted by too many educators. We must, as Leck suggests, move "forward into new opportunities for dialogue that can dramatically, dynamically, and subtly open vital new possibilities for more reflective and just practices of schooling" (p. 260).

NOTE

1. According to Denise Ottoson (2000), *intersexed* is "[t]he term preferred by people born with both female and male characteristics; the more commonly used term in history is hermaphrodite. Children born with obvious intersexed characteris-

tics are often operated on as an infant to remove whichever characteristics the family or surgeon decides should disappear. This may or may not coincide with which gender the child considers him/herself to be." *Transgenderism* is "a much debated term. It can be an umbrella to refer to all forms of thinking and behavior across gender lines. Transgender is also a catch phrase for people who don't quite fall into transvestite or transsexual categories." Here, I use *gay and lesbian, queer,* and *l/g/b/t/i/q people* interchangeably.

REFERENCES

Ada, A. (1995). *My name is Maria Isabel.* New York: Aladdin.

Avicolli, T. (1998). He defies you still: The memoirs of a sissy. In P. S. Rothenberg (Ed.), *Race, class, and gender in the United States: An integrated study,* Fourth edition (pp. 328-333). New York: St. Martins.

Bornstein, K. (1994). *Gender outlaw: On men, women, and the rest of us.* New York: Vintage.

Chasnoff, D. (producer/director) (1995). *It's elementary: Talking about gay issues in school* [Videotape]. Available from Women's Educational Media, New York.

Curtis, C. (1995). *The Watsons go to Birmingham—1963.* New York: Bantam Doubleday Dell.

dePaola, T. (1990). *Oliver Button is a sissy.* New York: Voyager.

dePaola, T. (2001). *Oliver Button is a star.* [Videotape] Available from TCGMC/ Oliver Project, 26 Ayers Road, Monson, MA 01057.

Elliot, M. (1996). Coming out in the classroom. *College English 58,* 693-708.

Elwin, R. and Lee, D. (1990). M. Paulse (Illus.) *Asha's mums.* Toronto, Ontario: Women's Press.

Kaeser, G. (1999). *Love makes a family.* Cambridge: University of Massachusetts Press.

Kennedy, J. (1998). *Lucy goes to the country.* Los Angeles, CA: Alyson.

King, J. and Schneider, J. (1999). Locating a place for gay and lesbian themes in elementary reading, writing, and talking. In W. Letts and J. Sears (Eds.), *Queering elementary education: Advancing the dialogue about sexualities and schooling,* (pp. 125-136). Lanham, MD: Rowman and Littlefield.

Leck, G. (1999). Afterword. In W. Letts and J. Sears (Eds.), *Queering elementary education: Advancing the dialogue about sexualities and schooling,* (pp. 257- 262). Lanham, MD: Rowman and Littlefield.

Lorber, J. (1998). The social construction of gender. In P. Rothenberg (Ed.), *Race, class, and gender in the United States: An integrated study,* Fourth edition (pp. 33-45). New York: St. Martin's.

Lorde, A. (1998). Age, race, class, and sex: Women redefining difference. In P. S. Rothenberg (Ed.), *Race, class, and gender in the United States: An integrated study,* Fourth edition (pp. 533-539). New York: St. Martin's.

Lowry, L. (1998). *Number the stars.* New York: Laurel Leaf.

Martino, W. (1999). "It's okay to be gay": Interrupting straight thinking in the English classroom. In W. J. Letts and J. T. Sears (Eds.), *Queering elementary education: Advancing the dialogue about sexualities and schooling* (pp. 137-149). Lanham, MD: Rowman and Littlefield.

Newman, L. (1989). *Heather has two mommies.* Los Angeles, CA: Alyson.

Ottoson, D. (2000). Transgender language and definitions. Available online at <http:/www.sexuality.org/l/incoming/trbasic.htm>.

Phelan, S. (1994). *Getting specific: Postmodern lesbian politics.* Minneapolis: University of Minnesota Press.

Ringold, F. (1996). *Tar Beach.* New York: Dragonfly Books.

Salisbury, G. (1994). *Under the blood red sun.* New York: Bantam Doubleday Dell.

Sears, J. (1999). Teaching queerly: Some elementary propositions. In W. J. Letts and J. Sears (Eds.), *Queering elementary education: Advancing the dialogue about sexualities and schooling* (pp. 3-14). Lanham, MD: Rowman and Littlefield.

Smith, B. (1999a). African American lesbian and gay history: An exploration. In B. Smith, *The truth that never hurts: Writings on race, gender, and freedom* (pp. 82-92). New Brunswick, NJ: Rutgers University Press.

Smith, B. (1999b). Homophobia: Why bring it up? In B. Smith, *The truth that never hurts: Writings on race, gender, and freedom* (pp. 111-115). New Brunswick, NJ: Rutgers University Press.

Taylor, M. (1991). *Roll of thunder, hear my cry.* New York: Puffin.

Valentine, J. (1994). *One dad, two dads, brown dad, blue dad.* Los Angeles, CA: Alyson.

Woodson, J. (1995a). *From the notebooks of Melanin Sun.* New York: Scholastic.

Woodson, J. (1995b). A sign of having been here. *The Horn Book* (November/December), 711-715.

Woodson, J. (1999). *The house you pass on the way.* New York: Laurel Leaf.

Chapter 15

A School-Based Program
to Improve Life Skills
and to Prevent HIV Infection
in Multicultural Transgendered Youth
in Hawaii

P. Jayne Bopp
Timothy R. Juday
Cloudia W. Charters

Unlike Western cultures, transgendered (TG) individuals, or māhū, have long played a familiar and traditional role in Polynesian culture (Besnier, 1994; Matzner, 2001). Hawaii is home to large numbers of male-to-female TG persons, 70 percent of whom are of Native Hawaiian descent (Odo and Hawelu, 2001). Possibly as a result of the cultural familiarity, many TG individuals in Hawaii begin their gender transition in adolescence, often much earlier than their counterparts in the continental United States (Matzner, 2001; Weiss and Bopp, 2001). While TG persons may be more familiar in Hawaii than other parts of the United States, this population clearly remains stigmatized and marginalized. Although many TG persons may eventually find legal employment, subsistence prostitution remains a viable form of work for many (Odo and Hawelu, 2001; Weiss and Bopp, 2001).

Westernization has degraded the role of the māhū in Hawaiian culture (Matzner, 2001). Thus, what was once a position of respect, embracing traditional healers and other socially valued persons, is now one associated with shame (Matzner, 2001; Weiss and Bopp, 2001). Today, mothers often defend their māhū children, while males in the family enforce Western standards of masculine behavior (Weiss and Bopp, 2001).

Polynesian youth who do come out to their families as "gay" are often steered toward feminine behavior and occupations. This traditional māhū role is more culturally comprehensible than male homosexuality, as many Polynesians equate the gay identity primarily with Western people (Weiss and Bopp, 2001). Other Polynesian males begin their coming-out process with a māhū identity and only later understand themselves as gay rather than TG (Weiss and Bopp, 2001). In contrast, the more familiar Western pattern of coming out for TG persons typically starts with a gay self-identity, ultimately evolving toward a TG self-concept (Gibb, 2000). Furthermore, while TG youth in the continental United States often express their identity as "really female" or as "female trapped in a male body," local youth usually identify as "T," a third and distinct category (Matzner, 2001; Weiss and Bopp, 2001).

Many transgendered persons are denied appropriate socialization opportunities due to transphobia—a pervasive and reflexive fear or hatred of transgender people—that may manifest itself in discrimination, harassment, or even violence. These youth are blocked from appropriate socialization because their fundamental gender identity is stifled. This prevents them from engaging in basic human activities such as using gender-appropriate rest rooms, playing with gender-appropriate toys, and wearing gender-appropriate clothes. Transgender individuals often internalize transphobia, contributing to the development of self-destructive attitudes and behaviors, including increased risk for HIV infection (Keatley et al., 2002). Most Hawaiian TG youth express an attitude of "accepting their fate" as social outcasts, fully expecting lifelong difficulties associated with it (Weiss and Bopp, 2001). These ostracized TG students are at high risk for dropping out of school, violence, drug use, subsistence prostitution, homelessness, HIV infection, and sexually transmitted diseases (Odo and Hawelu, 2001).

In 1992, Hawaii Transgender Outreach launched Chrysalis, an after-school drop-in group for TG youth, at a rural Oahu high school. Although promising, the project was short-lived due to lack of funding. Five years later, Life Foundation, an AIDS service organization, received funding from the Hawaii State Department of Health to provide HIV-prevention services to male-to-female transgender individuals on the island of Oahu. The Chrysalis program was reestablished in October 1997 for transgender and questioning youth at the same school. In the fall of 1999, a second group was started at an urban high school on Oahu.

Social workers played an important role in getting "buy in" from administrators at both high schools. The social workers also were responsible for the initial recruitment of program participants. Parental permission to participate was written in general terms about HIV prevention and school success. Once established, students within the program recruited other māhū and questioning classmates.

Chrysalis holds weekly after-school meetings on campus for about two hours. About thirty are held in a school year, with six to twelve students attending each meeting. Students prefer meeting in a closed, safe space to ensure confidentiality, although non-TG students are welcome. The group facilitator, April, is a twenty-year, postoperative TG health educator employed by the Life Foundation. She is also a college graduate and has been an HIV-prevention educator for over six years. As a peer of the TG youth, she has faced—and overcome—the challenges that these individuals encounter.

Chrysalis uses a harm-reduction approach as a way of working with high-risk individuals who may not be willing to abstain from harmful behaviors. The goal of this client-centered, nonjudgmental approach is to make incremental positive behavior changes that reduce harm without necessarily eliminating it.

Chrysalis group discussions focus on issues raised by the TG youth as well as topics proposed by the facilitator. Examples of group topics include anatomy, sex reassignment surgery, communication skills, decision-making skills, and values clarification. The facilitator is careful to help students separate out common adolescent angst from what is unique to their gender and sexual identity. Peer support and the use of peer role models are key elements. Successful adult TG role models (accountants, bankers, doctoral candidates) are guest speakers.

The objectives of Chrysalis are to

1. motivate students to stay in school and to succeed there;
2. improve feelings of safety and belonging in school, home, and the community;

3. help participants in building self-esteem, self-efficacy, and aspirations to a satisfying, healthy, meaningful, and productive lifestyle as adults; and
4. decrease participants' risk of HIV/STD infections.

To assess the effectiveness of Chrysalis, an evaluation study was conducted in 2001. Using quantitative and qualitative data, this analysis focused on nine factors related to the objectives: school participation, educational and career goals, self-esteem, friends and peer support, family, physical safety, sex reassignment surgery, alcohol and drug use, and safer-sex self-efficacy. This chapter details how Chrysalis members compared with non-Chrysalis TG youth on these nine factors and provides insight into how Chrysalis has empowered program participants and its importance in their lives. Given the few school-based programs in the United States for transgendered youth, these data have implications for educational practice not only in Hawaii but nationally.

METHODS

Evaluation participants were composed of nine Chrysalis members, nine TG youth without a history of participation in Chrysalis, and five key informants recruited from among school counselors and mental health professionals. The nine Chrysalis members were recruited for the evaluation from both current and past Chrysalis groups. Participation in Chrysalis for at least one year was an inclusion criterion for the evaluation. The non-Chrysalis TG youth were recruited among outreach contacts with no history of participation in Chrysalis. Individuals in this comparison group were matched as closely as possible by race/ethnicity and age.

The study team developed a written, self-administered, anonymous survey with thirty-nine closed-ended questions. This survey was administered to both Chrysalis members and comparison group members on high school campuses, at private homes, and on the beach. It included questions on demographics and the nine objective-related topics. The survey incorporated four scales with multiple questions answered on a four-point scale of 0 to 3 (strongly agree to strongly disagree). The Rosenberg Self-Esteem Scale (Rosenberg, 1965) includes ten questions. Higher self-esteem is reflected in a lower aggregate score, which can range from 0 to 30. Lower scores on three additional scales, each of which was constructed using multiple questions, also represented more positive outcomes. Scores on the educational plan scale, the scale measuring relationships with friends, and the scale measuring relationship with family could range from 0 to 3, respectively.

In addition, the nine Chrysalis members participated in a short, semistructured confidential interview with eleven open-ended questions. Key informants completed a different short, semistructured, confidential interview consisting of six open-ended questions. These tape-recorded interviews took place on high school campuses, over the telephone, and in private homes. Responses corresponding to specific objective-related topics were transcribed and grouped accordingly.

A twenty-five-dollar incentive was paid to Chrysalis members who completed both a survey and an interview. A fifteen-dollar incentive was paid to TG youth in the comparison group who completed the survey only. Key informants who completed an interview were not paid.

RESULTS

Demographics

The mean age of Chrysalis members was 16.5 years (SD = 1.24, range = 14-18), and the mean age of non-Chrysalis TG youth in the comparison group was 15.8 years (SD = 1.30, range = 13-17). Table 15.1 presents the race/ethnicity of Chrysalis and comparison group members. Most of the individuals in both groups were multiethnic, and all were of Pacific Islander and/or Asian descent. The only individuals from a single ethnic group were Samoans.

School Participation and Climate

All Chrysalis participants were attending school, including college and night school. Only four non-Chrysalis TG youth were in school; the other five had dropped out or had been expelled. Five Chrysalis members had not skipped school at all during the past year, while this

TABLE 15.1. Race/Ethnicity of Participants in Chrysalis Evaluation

	Chrysalis Group Members		Comparison Group Members	
	Number	Percent	Number	Percent
Native Hawaiian/Asian	2	22	2	22
Native Hawaiian/Black	1	11	1	11
Native Hawaiian/White	1	11	1	11
Samoan	3	33	2	22
Asian/Samoan	0	0	1	11
Asian/White	1	11	1	11
Asian/Hispanic	1	11	1	11
TOTAL	9	100	9	100

was true for only one non-Chrysalis TG youth. Seven Chrysalis members reported being teased less because of the program, and six said that other students were more respectful of them. Some students stated that it helped them to mingle with other students, to focus on school, and to deal more effectively with their anxieties. Fia, an eighteen-year-old who attended the rural high school, is one such student:

> There was this one boy who teased me a lot. Then he found out I was in the Chrysalis group. When I told him what it was about, he understood. After that, he didn't tease me. . . . If I was going to a class that I knew a lot of kids were going to tease me, I wouldn't go. After Chrysalis, I learned to just let the teasing go in one ear and out the other. I used to cut a lot of classes. If it weren't for Chrysalis, I wouldn't have graduated.[1]

Fia is currently in college.

Tita, a sixteen-year-old TG-identified youth from the urban high school, agreed:

> [E]ver since we started Chrysalis, new ideas came into my mind, and when they [boys] teased me, I started going right into their face and telling them straight up. . . . Like this one bully who was calling me *boto* sucker and sex fanatic. I just went up to

him and sat down next to him, and he was telling me, "Get away. Get away, you shit." And I just told him, "All the words you say to me go back to you and whatever you tell me I forgive you." And now he just tells me, "Hi."

But for Tita, not being harassed is not the same as being understood: "Some people still don't understand me, but now people don't harass me anymore or give me stink eye."

According to the key informants, this less harassment-filled environment contributed to improved school performance of some Chrysalis members. After joining the group, they became more focused and cared more about their academic work. School attendance dramatically improved for some members who had previously had serious attendance problems.

Educational and Career Goals

Chrysalis members appeared to be highly motivated to continue their education. Table 15.2 compares the educational goals of Chrysalis members with those in the comparison group. On a scale of 0 to 3 (strongly agree to strongly disagree), Chrysalis participants scored one full point better than nonparticipants—0.2 versus 1.2, respectively.[2]

TABLE 15.2. Mean Scores for Scales of Educational Plans, Self-Esteem, and Releationships with Friends and Family

	n	**Mean**	**SD**	**Range**
Educational Plans				
Chrysalis	9	0.2	0.36	0.0-1.0
Non-Chrysalis	9	1.2	1.00	0.0-3.0
Rosenberg Self-Esteem Scale				
Chrysalis	9	9.3	5.81	2.0-17.0
Non-Chrysalis	9	14.3	3.81	10.0-21.0
Relationships with Friends				
Chrysalis	9	0.6	0.83	0.0-2.5
Non-Chrysalis	9	1.6	0.74	0.7-2.8
Relationship with Family				
Chrysalis	9	1.3	0.80	0.3-3.0
Non-Chrysalis	9	2.0	0.66	1.2-2.8

Six members emphasized the importance of positive adult TG role models in shaping their educational and career aspirations. Three students said that they would not have attended college without Chrysalis; however, two said that Chrysalis did not influence their goals.

"It gave me more confidence," commented Eli, a soft-spoken fifteen-year-old from an inner-city high school. "I used to be a shy person and now I'm more open. If I hadn't gone to Chrysalis I wouldn't have gone to business school and stuff. I would have stayed home with my mom." A mental health provider referred Malia to Chrysalis. This sixteen-year-old from the rural high school attributed her educational motivation to April, the group facilitator, who "believes in me and sees potential in me." Malia continued:

> April is a transsexual like me. She relates more with us, and that makes me feel even more assured. . . . She's a successful woman, and it makes me feel like there is hope for me. . . . I plan to go to [college] and major in cosmetology or architecture; my goal is to be successful.

Another rural high school student, Carmen, summarized the unspoken assumptions that society has for TGs and how Chrysalis adults combat them:

> The TG role models opened my eyes and influenced me. They let me know . . . we can actually function in society as normal people with normal jobs and be respected. They gave inspiration and opened my doors and gave me another perspective on life. Before, I saw māhūs as just being prostitutes, hairdressers, or interior designers.

Due to an extremely unstable home life, this seventeen-year-old had dropped out of school her senior year after two years in Chrysalis. However, she returned to night school to complete her high school graduation requirements.

Self-Esteem and Suicidality

In general, Chrysalis members had higher self-esteem than comparison group members, as measured by the Rosenberg Self-Esteem Scale. Table 15.2 presents comparative mean scores and standard deviations for the two groups. There was a greater range among Chrysalis members; however, the group as a whole evidenced higher self-esteem. Although a causal relationship cannot be established empirically, interview data suggest otherwise.

Six members believed that Chrysalis helped them have greater confidence and to feel more supported. Four said it increased their self-esteem; four said that the program helped with self-acceptance/coming out. Participants volunteered that Chrysalis had opened them up, making them feel less isolated and less depressed. As Fia explained,

> The second or third week of Chrysalis, there was this session on being open. I needed to hear that. After that, I finally told everybody I was gay. . . . I got so much confidence. Chrysalis made me feel like I belonged, too. Chrysalis definitely helped my self-esteem.

Kunani "used to hide in the closet in front of certain people and Chrysalis would be like if you hide in the closet you will probably grow up to be in denial." This seventeen-year-old "figured maybe I should just open up now and try to figure out what I'm doing around here. Now that I've opened up, people have seen the real side of me." Before,

> I would act real māhū in front of the girls, but when I was around the boys, you have to act butch and stuff. But now I act māhū in front of the guys, and I'm surprised that certain guys actually accept me.

Four of the five key informants also saw the youth become more comfortable with themselves. Acknowledgment of the youth's gender identity, peer support, and providing community went a long way to affirming the self-esteem of program members. Something as simple as letting the members know that they were not crazy built confidence. Communication skills exercises, such as role-plays, emphasized how to be assertive with challenging situations and people without being aggressive or defensive. One risk factor for suicidal behavior is low self-esteem. Two students specifically stated how Chrysalis had kept them from this tragedy. Sixteen-year-old Pua faced many challenges in her rural community, including being developmentally delayed and a child in foster care:

> I was feeling like killing myself because of the way people treated me, the way they talked behind my back. I told April all of this, and she helped me. . . . She helped bring me up to a higher level, and I'm really thankful for how she helped my life. If I didn't have her, I would be dead or in the hospital. The truth is one time I tried to OD [overdose] on pills and ended up at the hospital for a few days because I didn't like my life. I wanted to dress like this, and people would tease me for it. It was really hard. Chrysalis helped me understand myself.

Three of the key informants cited Chrysalis as important in preventing suicide, prostitution, and drug use in this group. In Chrysalis, participants learned that what they were feeling was normal and got acknowledgment that it is hard growing up TG. For a TG, drug use is a common way to deal with these feelings and TGs often see prostitution as an avenue to validate gender identity, to socialize with the TG community, and to make money (Odo and Hawelu, 2001). When issues of peer support, self-esteem, and suicidal ideation are addressed, TG youth begin to look elsewhere for their self-validation.

Friends and Peer Support

According to the key informants, isolation and loneliness were common denominators among TG youth before Chrysalis; now, they have other TG youth as friends and a solid social support network. Chrysalis members were more likely to have better relationships with friends than non-Chrysalis members. Table 15.2 indicates members scored 0.6, and nonparticipants scored 1.6—a difference of a full point on the scale. According to Malia,

> [Chrysalis] definitely made me feel like I am not alone. It made me less depressed than I was before. April is very inspirational to me and makes me feel like there is hope for me, and that's why I live day by day. It has affected my emotional being. . . . I'm a little more confident than I was before. . . . I'm just being myself and living my life. I feel confident 'cause I have my

mom, my dad, and my family, plus Chrysalis plus other supporting friends.

Pua echoed the importance of Chrysalis during times of depression: "When you feel like killing yourself, you can come to group, and they ask you why and you can explain your life. You're more comfortable because they are all Ts." As Kunani described,

> When I get depressed, I know every Wednesday we have [Chrysalis], and its brought all us māhūs a lot closer. We knew each other, but we'd just say "Hi/Bye." But now we're really close. We talk to each other about our relationships or call each other and talk about what we did over the weekend.

Five students talked not only about the importance of April, the adult TG Chrysalis facilitator, but also the participating school social workers. Lani, a sixteen-year-old, TG-identified, urban student said,

> Chrysalis isn't like your parents who tell you you have to get good grades—they're different. They support you, and if you're having a hard time and you tell them, they will help you. Especially [the school workers] will tell you things your mom didn't tell you.

Tui, a fourteen-year-old urban student, thought that "the people in Chrysalis are really helpful; they're like a family. We talk to each other and also have advisors that help us." The experiences of these students underscore the usefulness of the Chrysalis program's emphasis on peer support in lessening loneliness and depression.

Family

Chrysalis members have better relationships with their families than comparison group members. Chrysalis members reported a lower mean score, 1.3 compared to 2.0 (Table 15.2), than comparison group members. Students such as Kunani shared that involvement in Chrysalis helped in interactions with their family members:

> I had a cousin who didn't like that I was fem. He told me that if I was going to be around him that I have to act like a boy. I told

April that and she . . . said if you stay in the closet you might "lose it" later and stuff like that. So, I told him one day that he either takes me now or he ain't going to see me no more. So we had, like, this big conversation. So that . . . helped a lot.

Fia described a powerful exchange with his parents:

My family used to call me names. I used to think about running away. One day they called me names all day. I thought about prostituting myself. When I talked to April, she told me about what that path would lead to. I didn't do it. Because of Chrysalis, I told my mom and my dad I was gay. After that, they apologized to me for calling me names. They understood me better 'cause every Samoan family has a "T" in it, and they never called me names again.

Malia commented:

My mom was going through her own battle . . . [and] I was going through my own battle. . . . She has a good heart, but she was kind of confused about what was going on with her child. . . . It has helped my mom understand, so I think Chrysalis has benefited me, my mom, my family, so it's good.

Families often have a difficult time accepting their TG children. Although many TG youth do not have the acceptance or stability they would like at home, key informants underscored that Chrysalis has been useful in improving participants' coping skills for family-related situations.

Physical Safety

Twice as many Chrysalis members (eight) than nonparticipants believed that they could stop someone from harassing them at school, in the neighborhood, or at home. These unwanted actions included name-calling, bullying, intimidation, sexual harassment, and physical violence.

According to the key informants, as Chrysalis members became more confident about who they were, there was a greater tolerance from other students. For example, Chrysalis students at the urban high school staged a drag show at a senior assembly. At the end of the year, a traditional part of the school's annual activities was an assembly where seniors presented a talent show. One segment included five Chrysalis members who put on a pageant, featuring hula dancing and a fashion show—all in drag. It was very well received by the other students, in large part because of the confidence level of the Chrysalis members. Kunani mentioned the event in her interview. When asked about Chrysalis helping with self-confidence, she replied, "Oh, yes, very much. For self-confidence, I felt like a black sheep even around the māhūs, but I took a big step and tried drag and then even put on a big show at school!" Kunani participated in the planning of the show and performed in it.

Sex Reassignment Surgery

Fewer Chrysalis participants used female hormones than TG youth in the comparison group. As shown in Table 15.3, only two Chrysalis members reported their use compared to seven nonparticipants. Both of the Chrysalis youth obtained them from a legal source (i.e., a physician); this was true of only three of the nonparticipants.

After joining Chrysalis and entering a supportive environment, there was a general feeling among members that there was no need to rush the process of becoming physically female. Because Chrysalis provided counseling on a broad range of issues, participants were able to see that not all of their problems were related to being TG. During group discussions, normal adolescent angst was brought out and separated from what is really related to being TG. When Chrysalis members entered the program, they thought that if they went through the physical transformation their problems would be over. Chrysalis provided them with a different perspective, and members concluded that physical transformation was not a fast solution. This supportive, nonjudgmental environment with positive adult TG role models allowed Chrysalis youth, including Tui, to explore their self-identity:

> Chrysalis . . . really brought us out to our real selves. I'm really happy and I think other students out there would be happier being their real selves regardless of their family or the public. . . . Being our self means talking the way we do, walking the way we do, and being the gender we want to be—female and every-

thing. I don't really want to go further with changing my body parts or anything, but as far as my personality goes, I think society should accept it.

Alcohol and Drug Use

For every type of drug and alcohol, fewer Chrysalis members reported use than did members of the comparison group (see Table 15.3). Eight comparison group members consumed alcohol, com-

TABLE 15.3. Hormone, Alcohol and Drug Use by Chrysalis Group (*n* = 9) and Comparison Group (*n* = 9)

	Number	Percent
Hormone use		
Chrysalis	2	22
Non-Chrysalis	9	89
Beer consumption		
Chrysalis	1	11
Non-Chrysalis	7	78
Any alcohol consumption		
Chrysalis	1	11
Non-Chrysalis	5	56
Cigarette smoking		
Chrysalis	4	44
Non-Chrysalis	7	78
Marijuana use		
Chrysalis	2	22
Non-Chrysalis	5	56
Crack use		
Chrysalis	0	0
Non-Chrysalis	3	33
Crystal methamphetamine use		
Chrysalis	1	11
Non-Chrysalis	5	56
Any hard drug use		
Chrysalis	1	11
Non-Chrysalis	5	56

pared with four Chrysalis members. Chrysalis members also had lower use of hard drugs (e.g., crack cocaine, cocaine, crystal methamphetamine) than comparison group members. Only one Chrysalis member reported using hard drugs in contrast to five comparison group members. Most of the comparison group members who used hard drugs were not in school. Neither group reported heroin use or injecting drug use. One Chrysalis student said, "I used to do a lot of drugs before, but when I started seeing April she told me the pros and the cons of that." Factual information about drug use was provided using a harm-reduction approach. Students, however, were not expected to abstain from drug use. Like the issue of sex, here the emphasis was on safer drug use.

Safer-Sex Self-Efficacy

More individuals in the Chrysalis group felt confident that they could successfully negotiate safer sex in a situation with someone who did not want to use a condom (eight members versus four non-members). Twice as many Chrysalis members (six) as nonparticipants felt confident they could refuse unsafe sex in a sexual situation.

April's peer status, nonjudgmental attitude, and ability to implement harm-reduction approaches made her effective. Once the facilitator accepts that group members will have sex—and likely not always safely—risk can be reduced. For many of these members, sex is also about having their gender identity and self-esteem validated, so with increased self-esteem there is decreased sexual (particularly unsafe) activities.

The interviews underscored the value of Chrysalis in promoting healthier relationships and safer sex. Five members stated that Chrysalis taught them how to properly use condoms and five reported their use. Four credited the program for enabling them to postpone relationships, practice monogamy, or abstain from sex. Malia explained:

> April told me there is always time for guys. She told me that education is first. At this point in my life, . . . I'd rather be single 'cause I'm doing a lot of soul-searching. I want to work on myself so I can get into a relationship with someone. Before Chrysalis, I was boy crazy. It changed my view.

Tita remarked:

> The most important thing that I learned from it was that if any-
> one forces you to have sex, don't think that it's good—it's bad.
> And that the person you have sex with has to respect you the
> way you want them to. . . . Before, I would just have sex and not
> think about it.

Carmen said of Chrysalis, "It really instilled in me the value of life
and using a condom if you're going to have sex. If I'm going to have
sex, I'm going to use condoms."

DISCUSSION

The Chrysalis group scored better than the comparison group for
every objective-related topic, thus providing preliminary evidence of
program effectiveness. Positive comments in the interviews from
Chrysalis members and key informants further support the program's
success. While causal relationships could not be established because
preintervention measurements were not taken and due to the small
sample sizes, Chrysalis is perceived as playing an important role in
improving the educational outcomes and life skills and in preventing
HIV/STD among TG youth.

The interviews provided insight into the program components critical to the success of Chrysalis. Members emphasized the importance
of positive adult TG role models, most notably the group facilitator,
April. Her effectiveness was largely attributable to several factors.
Using a harm-reduction approach, April's interactions with Chrysalis
members were client centered and nonjudgmental. She focused the
group on issues of importance to members—many of the same issues
she had experienced. Because she was an adult TG peer, was respected by other adults, and showed Chrysalis members respect,
April bonded with them. She also provided support to parents of TG
youth who sought her for activities, ranging from shopping for school
clothes to acting as intermediary between them and their child.

Peer support was another critical component. Before joining the
group, a common characteristic of every participant was loneliness.
Many of them felt that they were the only person with such feelings.
Through Chrysalis, they met others who shared similar concerns,

fears, and interests. Members organically developed a sense of community, support, and friendship through sharing in this group dynamic. This peer support enabled them to develop greater self-confidence and self-esteem.

Negative feedback about the program from members was minimal and ranged from the desire for more guest speakers to wanting more field trips. The key informants strongly supported the Chrysalis program, and all five said that it improved their comfort level and ability to work with this population. These school counselors and mental health professionals observed Chrysalis participants becoming better integrated into school, more comfortable with themselves, more confident, and more mature. Some credited Chrysalis with being instrumental in addressing suicidal ideation and other mental health issues.

A key implication of this study is that the needs of TG youth are not being met with current school support services, including many GSAs (gay-straight alliances) and similar school-based groups. Secondary school administrators and educators in the United States have largely ignored the needs of sexual minority youth—particularly transgender students. Much of this situation is likely due to stigma; however, even in progressive communities, school-based support services are typically inadequate to meet the unique needs of transgendered students. Chrysalis is not a gay students' group or a TG-straight or gay-straight alliance.

Although Chrysalis allows peers of TG students to participate (regardless of their sexual or gender identities), most participants are TG identified or questioning. *The preponderance of TG students and staff in any program designed to serve transgender youth is critical for its effectiveness.* The very specific issues facing TG youth coupled with their small numbers (at least compared to lesbian, gay, and bisexual [LGB] students) mean their voices may be lost in a broader GSA-like agenda. Furthermore, TG youth may not be as well accepted or willing to participate in larger groups primarily focused on sexual orientation. Chrysalis is a group expressly for TG youth coming to terms with gender identity, not sexual orientation. Chrysalis is effective because TG youth needs and issues are put first in a peer-supported environment.

Given the lack of support services for transgendered youth, the failure of school administrators and educators to consider their unique needs, as well as the general lack of information around working with

TG youth, especially those of color, both the findings of this study and the practical experiences of implementing Chrysalis may be of particular value for educators and policymakers.

In addition to focusing on the specific needs of TG youth in a peer-supportive environment, weekly meetings must be consistent. Establishing trust with this population is critical to success, and once the program is initiated students rely heavily on group support. Thus, canceling even one group in the school year can erode trust and cause harm to participants, especially those with mental health needs.

Participation by school social workers is another critical factor. These professionals provide "buy-in" from school administrators and teaching staff, and they act as a contact point for program referrals. Furthermore, their participation builds trust and demonstrates to participants that the school *does* care. Likewise, social workers' participation in Chrysalis allows them to better understand and serve these youth.

Critical to its success were its harm-reduction approach and voluntary participation. Using a Chrysalis-like program to punish students either by forcing them to attend (because they "need it") or by withholding them from attending group for disciplinary reasons (e.g., poor grades, truancy) risks damaging the therapeutic group dynamics. Abstinence from sex, criminal activity, and substance use is not a requirement (or expectation) for participation. As a student-centered group, addressing the needs and issues raised by the participants is primary; the agenda of the facilitator or school is secondary. Only by allowing students to speak freely about the reality of their lives can educators begin to understand and address the complex challenges they face.

Educators need to assess how best to respond to the needs of their TG and questioning students. In Hawaii, due to cultural factors, TG students come out at a younger age than their counterparts in the continental United States (Matzner, 2001; Weiss and Bopp, 2001). Because of this difference, establishing a stand-alone, Chrysalis-like program in many high schools may be unrealistic. However, in schools with GSA programs and where a sufficient number of TG or questioning students are visible, educators must welcome their presence and assess the viability of forming a separate TG group. Educators must also be willing to work with TG students who do not feel comfortable even in a Chrysalis-like group. Where no GSA program exists, educators must be aware that the challenges facing TG and questioning students are different from their LGB peers. Knowledge about how to meet their unique needs is critical.

A program like Chrysalis, because it occurs during a critical period in a transgender adolescent's life, may reap lifelong benefits. As Fia put it, "I never thought I would go to college. Even from elementary school days, my only hope was to just graduate. Those two years in Chrysalis were the most important years of my life."

NOTES

1. In presenting quotations, actual names have been changed in order to protect their confidentiality.

2. The data allow for comparisons of the two groups but not for analyses of causation, because data for the two groups were not collected prior to the intervention. Due to the small sample sizes, no testing for statistical significance was possible.

REFERENCES

Besnier, N. (1994). Polynesian gender liminality through time and space. In G. Herdt (Ed.), Third sex, third gender (pp. 285-328). New York: Zone.

Gibb, S. (2000). Pastoral care with transgender people. Unitarian Universalist Association, Boston, MA. Available online at <www.uua.org/obgltc/resource/tgpc.pdf>.

Keatley, J., Nemoto, T., Operario, D., and Soma, T. (2002). *The impact of transphobia on HIV risk behaviors among male-to-female transgenders in San Francisco.* San Francisco: AIDS Research Institute, University of California.

Matzner, A. (2001). *O au no keia: Voices from Hawaii's māhū and transgender communities.* Philadelphia, PA: Xlibris.

Odo, C. and Hawelu, A. (2001). Eo na māhū o Hawai'i: The extraordinary health needs of Hawai'i's māhū. *Pacific Health Dialog, 8,* 327-334.

Rosenberg, M. (1965). *Society and adolescent self-image.* Princeton, NJ: Princeton University Press.

Weiss, A. and Bopp, P. (2001). Transgendered adolescents in multicultural Hawai'i. Paper presented at the 48th Annual Meeting of the American Academy of Child and Adolescent Psychiatry, Honolulu, Hawai'i, October 23-28.

Chapter 16

Describing Roles That Gay-Straight Alliances Play in Schools: From Individual Support to School Change

Pat Griffin
Camille Lee
Jeffrey Waugh
Chad Beyer

Following highly publicized events of violence in schools ranging from shootings to sexual harassment and bullying, parents and K-12 educators have increasingly focused their attention on school safety. Violence and harassment directed at lesbian, gay, bisexual, and transgender (LGBT) students are embedded in the broader educational concern. Research on LGBT students in schools overwhelmingly documents the discrimination and harassment they face in hostile school climates (Bochenek and Brown, 2001; Harris, 1997; Herr, 1999; Kosciw and Cullen, 2001; Mufioz-Plaza, Quinn, and Rounds, 2002; Reis, 1999; Russell, Bohan, and Lilly, 2000).

Though many LGBT young people endure a hostile school environment, there is a national movement to address their needs. National advocacy organizations such as the Gay, Lesbian and Straight Education Network (GLSEN), Parents, Families and Friends of Lesbians and Gays (PFLAG), and the American Civil Liberties Union (ACLU) also provide resources to school officials. Several national education organizations such as the National Education Association and the National School Boards Association have passed declarations

The authors would like to thank the Institute for Gay and Lesbian Strategic Studies, the Annie E. Casey Foundation, and the Ford Foundation for their generous support of this project.

of support for gay, lesbian, and bisexual students and have taken active roles in addressing this underserved group in schools.

Moreover, recent court decisions in several states have ruled that school districts failing to address antigay harassment and discrimination are liable for substantial monetary damages (Press, 1996, 2002). Eight states (Wisconsin, Minnesota, Massachusetts, Connecticut, California, Washington, New Jersey, and Vermont) have enacted legislation prohibiting discrimination and harassment on the basis of sexual orientation against students in schools. (Only the California and Minnesota laws include gender identity/expression.)

Staff training on LGBT youth issues, formation of school-based clubs called gay-straight alliances (GSAs), development of inclusive nondiscrimination policies, and curriculum inclusion evidence different approaches to addressing LGBT issues in schools. School-based GSAs are the most visible and widely adopted strategies. According to GLSEN, more than 1,000 school-based GSAs are active in 47 states. The dramatic increase in GSAs over the past ten years throughout the United States demonstrates the interest in and need for such groups.

Though both community-based conservative religious groups and some school personnel have resisted the formation of GSAs, the courts have consistently ruled in favor of students' rights to form these school-based clubs. The Federal Equal Access Act, originally designed to protect the rights of Christian students to participate in school-based Bible study clubs, now protects the rights of LGBT students and their friends to form GSAs. Although a burgeoning research literature documents the hostile school climate that LGBT youth face, recent research studies (Doppler, 2000; Griffin and Ouellett, 2002; Lee, 2002; Mayberry, 1997; McCready, 2000; Ouellett, 1999; Szalacha, 2001) examine what schools are doing to become safer for LGBT students and the impact on school climate and individual students.

Emerging evidence confirms that school-based student groups such as GSAs can play a role in how LGBT students and their friends perceive themselves in relationship to the school. Lee (2002) reported that GSA membership had a positive impact on students' academic performance, enhanced their sense of physical safety in the school, increased their perceived ability to contribute to society, and contributed to a greater sense of belonging to the school community. These results are consistent with Mayberry's 1997 study, which found that

GSA membership played an important role in "empowering the daily lives of a group of previously marginalized" students (p. 1).

Fewer studies focus on how GSAs may affect school climate, but two are notable. Doppler (2000) concluded that GSAs challenged silence and increased visibility of LGB issues in school, replaced isolation with connection for GSA members, provided opportunities for positive risk taking, and contributed to a new vision for school climate and culture. Similarly, Szalacha (2001) reported that schools with GSAs were significantly more likely than those that did not have them to be "welcoming" places for sexual minority students. Students in schools with GSAs were three times more likely to agree that LGB students can be open about their sexuality at school and were significantly less likely to hear antigay slurs in school on a daily basis.

These two studies invite more in-depth exploration of what kind of institutional functions GSAs play. Thus, the purpose of our qualitative study is to better understand whether and how GSAs become institutionalized in schools as part of a comprehensive organizational plan to become safe places for LGBT students.

Although GSAs may play a role in making schools safer and more inclusive for all students, research on school change indicates that the potential positive effects of GSAs are most likely to be long-lasting when they are part of a broad, ongoing, organization-level plan to affect institutional policies, programming, and practices (Fullan, 1991; Jackson and Holvino, 1998; LeCompte, 2000; Ouellett, 1999). Individual students and staff come and go. Without change at all levels of a school's organizational structure, the gains of any one year may be lost when GSA members graduate or club advisors retire. Understanding what GSAs do and how their activities are or are not integrated into other efforts to address safety issues is key in understanding the complexities of addressing gender and sexuality in schools.

SETTING, PARTICIPANTS, DATA COLLECTION, AND ANALYSIS

In 1993, Massachusetts became the first state to sponsor a safe schools program (SSP) situated in the state Department of Education (DOE). SSP provided support and resources to high schools as they acted on four DOE recommendations designed to make schools safe places for lesbian and gay students (transgender and bisexual students were not specifically addressed in the recommendations). Over ten years, many high schools across the state have participated in some aspects of the SSP. These activities include training school-based staff, organizing GSAs, applying for small annual DOE grants for GSA activities, and sending selected staff and students to DOE conferences focused on making schools safe for LGBT students. Of these activities, formation of school-based GSAs quickly emerged as the centerpiece of the Safe Schools Program with almost 200 sponsoring high schools.

Twenty-two high schools that have participated in the Massachusetts Safe Schools Program compose the sample for this study. Initially, we obtained a list of schools participating in various aspects of the SSP from the DOE. From this, a diverse purposive sample of schools was selected on the basis of community characteristics (rural, suburban, and urban), racial/ethnic and economic profile of the school community, school size, and regional distribution.

To develop an in-depth description, our research team employed qualitative methods that included interviews, observations, and questionnaires focused on addressing the primary goal of describing what organizational level change efforts were undertaken in each school. One or two researchers visited each school five to ten times over the course of two to three months.

In each school, members of the research team interviewed GSA advisors and principals, as well as other key staff identified by the GSA advisor and principal as playing a role in efforts to become safe for LGBT students. Depending on the school, these interviews included superintendents, guidance counselors, teachers, parents, and community members. Staff or community members who did not support the school's efforts to address LGBT issues were interviewed when other interviewees identified their opposition. Researchers also attended school activities and collected relevant written documents such as GSA displays, student handbooks, nondiscrimination policies, and curriculum materials. School policies about researcher interactions with students varied. In some schools, we attended GSA meetings or conducted group interviews with GSA members. In others, we distributed anonymous questionnaires to students participating in the GSA. Student questionnaires and interviews focused on students' school experiences and perceptions of the school climate for LGBT students and allies. A few schools would not permit any contact with students or required parental permission (this was a problem when parents did not know or approve of their children's participation in the GSA).

Interviews and observations were transcribed and, with questionnaire data, coded by using a guide developed by the research team based on initial readings of all interviews. The research team met weekly to discuss data collection, code identification, and analysis of the data. Based on this analysis, a profile was developed for each school, as well as the identification of cross-school themes related to organizational efforts.

ROLES GSAs PLAY IN SCHOOLS

Our analysis identified four roles that GSAs in the twenty-two schools played: providing counseling and support; providing safe space; serving as a primary vehicle for raising awareness, increasing visibility, and educating about LGBT issues in school; and becoming a part of broader school efforts for raising awareness, increasing visibility, and educating about LGBT issues in school. Each of these roles is discussed in the following sections and data from the schools are presented to support the creation of these categories (see Table 16.1).

Counseling and Support

GSAs that played a counseling and support role did not function as a typical school club, but were places (usually the school counselor's office) where students could meet together or individually with the GSA advisor. Although participants in the school referred to this group as a GSA, the focus was on assisting individual students who were dealing with sexual identity or gender identity issues. Thus, the GSA advisor was a school counselor. Safety issues in these schools were defined as psychological (e.g., isolation, suicide, depression, and identity confusion among LGBT or questioning students), and the problem was defined primarily as a matter of individual adjustment. Consequently, these GSAs did not plan or participate in educa-

TABLE 16.1. Roles GSAs Play in Schools

Role	Characteristics
Counseling and support for LGBT students	Invisible
	Individual counseling
	Internal
	Focus on LGBT students
	Safety: psychological support for LGBT students
Safe space for LGBT students and friends	Invisible/visible
	Individual support
	Internal
	Focus on LGBT students and friends
	Safety: social support for LGBT students and friends
Primary vehicle for education and awareness in school	Visible
	Individual rights
	External
	Focus on LGBT students and friends
	Safety: tolerant school climate
Part of broader efforts to educate and raise awareness in school	Visible
	Individual rights and organization change
	External
	Focus on LGBT students and friends
	Safety: tolerant school climate

tional or awareness activities that engaged other members of the school community.

Two school GSAs in our study (A and N) played this counseling and support role. Staff members in School A told us that LGBT issues were not addressed and that LGBT staff members did not feel safe identifying themselves. Students who participated in the GSA believed that the school climate was too hostile for an openly identified student club that focused on LGBT issues. Instead, the students formed a group that dealt with sexual orientation without calling attention to themselves, choosing the name ESP (Educate, Support, Protect). The school adjustment counselor agreed to serve as the ESP advisor but did not feel supported by the administration, colleagues, or the community. Initially, the group was limited to one hour of support a week when students were able to go to the counselor's office during an activity period. Essentially a secret society in the school, ESP did not participate in or plan any activities other than their weekly meetings where, according to the adjustment counselor, "the kids knew that they had a place for one hour on Tuesdays where they would be safe."

For its first three years, the GSA at School N also organized as an underground group. Here the adjustment counselor was asked by the school principal to be the advisor on her first day on the job. This GSA advisor entered the role "with my therapist hat on." She saw herself working with a "clinical population" and believed that her therapist role influenced the tone of the very small group. As in School A, all GSA activities were not public; the goal was to create a social gathering place where students could safely meet.

"Safe" Space

GSAs providing "safe" space were official student clubs and functioned similarly to other school clubs. Unlike GSAs serving a counseling and support role, safe space GSAs were visible through public address announcements and posters in hallways that invited the student body to participate. These clubs, however, did not typically include events for the school community or for students who were not GSA affiliated. The goal of these GSAs was to provide a place and time where students could socialize and talk with other students who shared their LGBT interests. Typical GSA activities included watching videos, eating pizza, having guest speakers at meetings, or discussing school safety. GSA members also attended events outside of school, including DOE Safe Schools conferences, Youth Pride marches, and movies or plays with LGBT themes. Adults in these schools considered the GSA's visible presence an important statement of inclusion and potential support for any students who needed it even if the GSA was a small or inactive group.

We qualify our use of "safe" in reference to these GSAs because some staff and students did not consider the GSA safe for all LGBT students. The members of many GSAs in this study were predominantly white heterosexual girls, LGBT or questioning students who did not identify themselves in GSA meetings, and other students who did not easily "fit in" to student social circles regardless of their sexuality. Furthermore, in most of our schools, LGBT youth did not identify themselves or discuss specific personal issues in GSA meetings. Activities centered on providing members with mutual support, empowerment, and education about LGBT matters. Consequently, some LGBT students did not feel "safe" in the GSA. Consistent with other research, LGBT students of color, openly identified LGBT students, and LGBT or questioning students seeking counseling and support did not always see the GSA as a place that met their needs (McCready, 2000).

In our study, GSAs in six schools functioned as safe spaces. School A had initially played a counseling and support role, but with a new principal and the addition of several young teachers, a few of whom openly identified as lesbians, the GSA assumed a different role. Interviewees in School A described how LGBT issues were being addressed in a positive, supportive, and much more visible way: an antigay graffiti incident in the school was discussed in every homeroom and more heterosexual staff members were stepping forward to express support for addressing LGBT concerns. One lesbian and one bisexual teacher restarted the GSA as a student club rather than as a counseling and support group. Its new activities would provide a safe space for students who chose to come to GSA meetings rather than sponsor activities for the larger school. The advisors sent a letter to each faculty member describing what the GSA was and why it was important. They also included GSA meeting flyers for classroom posting.

In contrast, the GSA advisor at School K did not feel supported by her principal. Though small, the GSA met regularly and they carried a school banner in a local city LGBT Pride Parade. They also participated in dances with GSAs from other city high schools and attended DOE-sponsored Safe School conferences. School K's GSA was mainly a social support group, though members were planning ways to raise awareness of LGBT issues in their school. They took part in a citywide Safe Schools Week by asking individual schoolmates to sign a pledge to discourage antigay actions and by providing safe zone stickers for teachers to post in their classrooms.

The GSA in School I was quite visible in the school through meeting and event announcements, a bulletin board in a main hallway, and T-shirts they sold with a rainbow and "Respect for All" logo. The GSA also attended DOE-sponsored conferences, the Youth Pride march, and the state GLSEN conference. The focus of GSA events, according to the advisor, was to build a team or family. Her goal was to plan enjoyable activities that would attract students who might not otherwise think of joining the GSA. They went on an annual bike trip and had sleepovers in the gym to which other GSAs were invited for activities such as wall climbing, volleyball, soccer, and eating. During the evening, the advisor led a discussion about LGBT issues or school safety.

Primary Vehicle for Raising Awareness, Providing Education, Increasing Visibility of LGBT Issues in the School

In these schools, the GSA was a recognized student club with regular meetings. Activities were social, educational, and/or political in nature. As in schools where the GSA was primarily a safe space, the GSA was visible through public address announcements, posters, and bulletin boards. The distinguishing characteristic of these GSAs, however, was the lead role they played in calling attention to LGBT safety issues. Although adults were supportive, school programming on LGBT topics was initiated by the GSA and was the primary way that LGBT issues were addressed. If staff training occurred, the GSA had lobbied for it and often participated in it. The GSA planned schoolwide events such as assemblies or exhibits on LGBT topics. The GSA visited classes to talk to their peers about the state student rights law that prohibited discrimination on the basis of sexual orientation.

These activities increased the profile of LGBT issues (but not necessarily individuals) in the school. GSA meetings were also safe spaces for members to socialize and plan activities with other students who shared their LGBT concerns and interests. Nine GSAs in our study were the primary vehicle for LGBT education, visibility, and awareness in their schools.

The GSA at School P sponsored a Gay Awareness Week during which information about the history, culture, and current status of LGBT life was shared with the student body each day during morning announcements. Members also gave ribbons to students and staff to wear that read "Homophobia Kills."

School J's GSA coordinated a presentation to three classes with speakers from a university LGBT Center and, with a DOE grant, purchased a small collection of resources for the school library. During their Safe Schools Week, members sponsored a poster contest open to all students and collected signatures of classmates pledging to stop antigay name-calling. At one faculty meeting, they even served cake to teachers in thanks for their support.

The GSA at School L spearheaded efforts to add LGBT content to the school library and sponsored two after-school videos on LGBT-related topics for the general student body and faculty. They also sold T-shirts with their own logo and the message "Respect for All." At School B, the GSA put posters in the library highlighting gay historical figures, sponsored an assembly for the school with gay and lesbian speakers, organized an LGBT book exhibit in the library, and passed out pink triangles to students and staff on National Coming Out Day.

Many of the GSAs in this category participated in a wide variety of visibility activities, including hanging a rainbow flag in the cafeteria, putting up posters all over the school describing the GSA and inviting students to meetings, and asking teachers to put up safe zone stickers in their classrooms.

Part of Broader School Efforts for Raising Awareness and Providing Education to Make School Safe for LGBT Students in School

The GSAs in these schools were a notable part of broader efforts to address LGBT issues. These wider school efforts were initiated and carried out by other school or community members or groups. Sometimes these activities were cosponsored by the GSA, but other activities occurred without GSA sponsorship. The key difference was that, unlike the previous category, these GSAs were not acting as the primary vehicle for addressing LGBT issues. Some schools established a standing district or school-based Safe Schools Task Force of staff, parents, and students. These committees sponsored community and school-based events such as the Love Makes a Family photo exhibit, diversity days that included LGBT topics, or administering school climate surveys to students. Other steps not prompted by the GSA included staff development programs on LGBT issues mandated by the principal and inclusion of LGBT curriculum content in classes. Staff-initiated activities included interventions to stop antigay harassment, education about and enforcement of student rights law and harassment policies, inclusion of domestic partner benefits for LGBT staff, and programs for same-sex parents.

Among the twenty-two schools in our study, five GSAs adopted this role. School E had a safe schools committee that maintained strong connections with the DOE. Working in partnership with the principal, this committee adopted a statement of support for the legal rights of LGBT students in the student handbook. It was also distributed to the faculty. The principal's strong advocacy was a key component of the GSA's success in School E. She reported that the GSA action plan was written into the overall school plan. When faculty made inappropriate comments regarding LGBT students or issues, the principal used school policy to redirect them. She believed that heterosexism was similar to racism and thought it was important for students to have openly lesbian and gay teachers.

School H formed a safe schools task force consisting of staff, parents, and students. Among other LGBT projects, they conducted a survey of parents' attitudes about LGBT issues, sponsored staff training for teachers and guidance counselors, sponsored the Love Makes a Family photo exhibit, and used DOE grant money to purchase LGBT books for the library. The district health coordinator, who provided leadership and direction for the task force, was instrumental in making the school safe for LGBT students. The task force supported GSA activities, such as passing out pink triangles to teachers to wear prior to the photo exhibit. Motivated by GSA students, several teachers also posted safe zone stickers in their classrooms. A vocal but small community group opposed these activities, but administrators defended them as important in making the school safe for all students.

The GSA in School F was started by the librarian after he became involved with the school's safe schools team and attended a DOE training. The team coordinated trainings for administrators and faculty. Other student groups also encouraged discussion of LGBT issues. For example, the Drama Team performed a gay-themed play called *Removing the Glove.* Teachers also promoted a more inclusive curriculum. A biology teacher included LGBT issues in genetics and biological diversity. A social studies teacher discussed LGBT stereotypes and labeling in current events and in the context other minorities' experiences.

The GSA in School O began in 1993. The school had already been including "homosexuality" as part of a peer support program affiliated with the counseling staff. Early on, a group of faculty, staff, and community members formed a districtwide Safe Schools Task Force. In addition, the DOE facilitated several mandatory staff trainings at the school.

The school administration, school committee, and superintendent pledged their full support of School O's participation in the SSP. The principal became an avid backer, speaking on panels to encourage administrators from other schools to address LGBT issues. He said, "[It is] easy for me to take the lead on these issues when I have the support of the school committee and the superintendent." The GSA advisor secured funds from DOE grants each year and the Safe and Drug Free Schools Coordinator obtained other grants on a regular basis. She believed that, even if DOE funding were to run out, the district would provide money for the GSA: "I think we would still be full speed ahead—and we are deeply committed to the issue."

One of the most striking attributes of School O was its deep connection with a community that publicizes itself as a diverse place to live. With approximately 100 student members and regular announcements of its activities, the GSA at School O was highly visible. A large GSA bulletin board, featuring student poetry, help-line resources, and posters about antigay harassment, greeted students as they entered the school. The GSA also brought the Shared Heart exhibit to the school for general display. Several adults observed, "Nobody looks twice if same-sex dates show up for the prom." GSAs from other schools were even welcomed at that significant event.

Several yearly GLBT-related events have become institutionalized. Each first-year class attends an assembly on harassment in which homophobia is a main topic. In addition, the GSA sponsors a Day of Dialogue for students from School O and GSAs from other schools, during which a rainbow flag is prominently displayed in front of the school. A panel of invited speakers addresses a variety of LGBT-related topics and is followed by small group discussions.

DISCUSSION

The four roles that GSAs played in the twenty-two schools in our study are general descriptions of how these student groups were (or were not) connected to overall school efforts to become safe for LGBT students. Because GSA roles can change over time, these descriptions are best read as "snapshots" in the school's history. Changes often occurred as students graduated and new groups of GSA members with different interests took over leadership. Shifts in the number of GSA members from year to year also affected its role. In some cases, the GSA became inactive and then was reactivated by new students or faculty advisors.

In a few cases, GSAs assumed more than one role in their schools. For example, we identified the GSA in School G as safe space. However, this GSA also organized an annual educational program for incoming ninth-graders. These GSA role transitions and shifts have implications for the long-term efficacy of safe schools efforts.

Benefits and Shortcomings of the Roles GSAs Play

Each role that a GSA plays has benefits and shortcomings. GSAs that provide counseling and support help individual students work through identity issues and the accompanying stresses. However, these programs do not address organizational change and school climate regarding LGBT issues or acknowledge their importance to the rest of the school.

In schools where the GSA is safe space, its members can meet with peers who share similar values. LGBT and questioning students can develop support and a sense of community that can break down their frequent isolation. For heterosexual members, the GSA can be a vehicle for acting on the value of inclusion and for supporting LGBT family members and friends. GSA visibility can "normalize" LGBT issues and remind the rest of the school that LGBT students are a part of the community. However, when a safe space GSA is the only LGBT-related school resource, students may miss needed counseling services. Because the GSA's membership is mixed—heterosexual, gay, bisexual, transgender, questioning, or not identified—addressing their diverse interests in one club also is difficult. Some LGBT students concerned about confidentiality do not consider a GSA, often composed mostly of heterosexual allies, to be safe. In addition, the safe space role, while providing a haven for some students, does not address schoolwide climate or safety concerns.

When describing GSAs as safe spaces or support groups, it is important to ask the question, "Safe and supportive for whom?" GSAs are not static "one-size-fits-all" clubs. There is no easy way to meet the changing needs of all students who might benefit from participation, but noticing who does and does not participate is a first step to identify ways that schools can provide safety and support for students who do not find either in their GSA. In our study, for example, many GSA members were white students and because intersections of LGBT identity with race were rarely broached, students of color might not feel safe in these clubs.

Schools in which the GSA is the primary vehicle for raising awareness, visibility, tolerance, and understanding about LGBT issues can be empowering for heterosexual and LGBT members and can provide valuable lessons in taking social action consistent with democratic values. For LGBT youth, being part of such a group can help them overcome persistent isolation and victimization in school. However, when the GSA is the sole agent for such activism, it is questionable how much systemic or even personal change can occur or continue. Without participation and leadership of other adults and students, addressing LGBT issues can become marginalized.

In some of the schools we visited, GSA advisors and members expressed concern about dwindling numbers, a lack of follow-through among members, the graduation of a dynamic leader, or the retirement of a devoted advisor. When the GSA is the primary reform agent, any of these factors can have a devastating effect on safe school efforts. In the space of one academic year, a school can go from a high level of activity and achievement to silence, depending on the vitality of the GSA.

When GSAs play a role as part of broader systemic efforts, they typically focus on the membership's needs as only one part of their mission. For example, in School H, the Safe Schools Task Force took responsibility for planning schoolwide education and awareness activities and for arranging staff-development programs. Although this GSA participated in some of the former, it was not solely responsible for this role in the school. Members could enjoy primarily a safe space and take on a more public educational role when they chose to.

GSA members could work in partnership with the task force members and rely on them for support. If GSA membership and visibility in such a school decreases from one year to the next, schoolwide activities are still assured.

Regardless of the roles played by GSAs, a limitation of many efforts is their focus on changing individual behavior and awareness rather than making more substantial institutional changes. Although individual change is an important first component of making schools safe for LGBT students, sustained changes in school climate and structure require a systemic approach. Research on school change indicates that GSAs would be most effective as part of a broad ongoing effort to make schools safe and welcoming for all students, staff, and families (Fullan, 1991; Sarason, 1971).

All the schools in our study focused primarily on improving safety for LGBT students and their friends regardless of the roles that GSAs played or their degree of organizational change focus. As such, these schools can be described as examples of what Kumashiro (2000, pp. 26, 31) called "education for the other" and "education about the other." GSAs playing a counseling and support role or a safe space role focused on the needs of LGBT students and their friends (education *for* the other). GSAs that were either the primary vehicle for or part of broader school efforts to raise awareness about LGBT issues among the entire school community are examples of education *about* the other. The focus on the safety of GSA members, however, does not necessarily address larger patterns of heterosexism, sexism, or racism embedded in school policy, practice, and programming. Demanding tolerance and respect for gender and sexual nonconformity among students may help to make schools safer for them, but does not challenge the norms and expectations that underlie violence, harassment, or discrimination. None of the schools or their GSAs in our study addressed such issues as how heterosexism and gender oppression privilege heterosexual and gender conforming students or marginalize LGBT students. Challenging gender and sexuality norms and their effects on all students is perhaps a next step in addressing LGBT issues in schools. This shift in focus would constitute what Kumashiro (2000, p. 35) called "education that is critical of privileging and othering."

Cultural norms are enforced in both the explicit and hidden curricula and in school policy, practice, and programming. Given the major importance of schools in socializing young people, it is important to examine and dismantle institutional structures that support oppressive norms of gender and sexuality. Otherwise, these norms are taken for granted as part of a "neutral" context for safe school efforts.

The liberal "safety and tolerance" paradigm challenges schools to address institutional policies and practices as well as individual beliefs and behaviors that discriminate against LGBT students and limit their civil rights. Because underlying gender and sexuality norms are not challenged, the safety and tolerance focus has been less threatening for schools to adopt. Indeed, some schools and communities find even this approach too radical.

Perhaps, as a first step, the school safety and tolerance paradigm is the best place to begin addressing LGBT issues. There is no doubt that student lives have been saved and school climates have been improved when this paradigm guides schools' efforts to become safer for LGBT students, staff, and families. The challenge is to appreciate the value of safety and tolerance as a beginning, but not as an end. For schools to become places where social justice values are lived through school policy and individual behavior, safety and tolerance are minimal goals. Schools will need to move beyond these goals to a more comprehensive examination of heterosexism and gender oppression and their effects on all members of the school community.

REFERENCES

Bochenek, M. and Brown, A. (2001). *Hatred in the hallways: Violence and discrimination against lesbian, gay, bisexual, and transgender students in U.S. schools.* New York: Human Rights Watch.

Doppler, J. (2000). A description of gay/straight alliances in the public schools of Massachusetts. Unpublished doctoral dissertation, University of Massachusetts, Amherst.

Fullan, M. (1991). *The new meaning of educational change.* New York: Teachers College Press.

Griffin, P. and Ouellett, M. (2002). *Going beyond gay-straight alliances to make schools safe for lesbian, gay, bisexual, and transgender students.* Amherst, MA: Institute for Gay and Lesbian Strategic Studies.

Harris, M. (Ed.) (1997). *School experiences of gay and lesbian youth: The invisible minority.* Binghamton, NY: The Haworth Press.

Herr, K. (1999). Institutional violence in the everyday practice of school: The narrative of a young lesbian. *Journal for a Just and Caring Education, 5*(3), 242-255.

Jackson, B. and Holvino, E. (1998). Developing multicultural organizations. *Journal of Religion and the Applied Behavioral Sciences, 9*(2), 14-19.

Kosciw, J. and Cullen, M. (2001). *National school climate survey: The school-related experiences of our nation's lesbian, gay, bisexual, and transgender youth.* New York: Gay, Lesbian and Straight Education Network.

Kumashiro, K. (2000). Toward a theory of anti-oppressive education. *Review of Educational Research, 70*(1), 25-54.

LeCompte, M. (2000). Standing for just and right decisions. *Education and Urban Society, 32*(3), 413-429.

Lee, C. (2002). The impact of belonging to a high school gay/straight alliance. *The High School, 85*(3), 13-26.

Mayberry, M. (1997). Lessons in challenging homophobia in schools: The East High School gay-straight student alliance. Paper presented at the Society for the Study of Social Problems Conference.

McCready, L. (2000). When fitting in isn't an option, or why black queer males at a California high school stay away from Project 10. In K. Kumashiro (Ed.), *Troubling intersections of race and sexuality* (pp. 37-54). Lanham, MD: Rowman and Littlefield.

Mufioz-Plaza, C., Quinn, S., and Rounds, K. (2002). Lesbian, gay, bisexual, and transgender students: Perceived social support in the high school. *The High School Journal, 85*(4), 52-63.

Ouellett, M. (1999). A multicultural organization development examination of school-based change strategies to address the needs of gay youth. Unpublished doctoral dissertation, University of Massachusetts, Amherst.

Press, A. (1996). School to pay gay man $900,000. *Wisconsin State Journal,* November 21.

Press, A. (2002). School district settles harassment suit with gay teenager. Associated Press (Lexis Nexis). January 17.

Reis, B. (1999). *They don't even know me: Understanding anti-gay harassment and violence in schools.* Seattle: Safe Schools Coalition of Washington State.

Russell, G., Bohan, J., and Lilly, D. (2000). Queer youth: Old stories, new stories. In S. Jones (Ed.), *A sea of stories: The shaping power of narrative in gay and lesbian cultures* (pp. 69-92). Binghamton, NY: The Haworth Press.

Sarason, S. (1971). *The culture of schools and the problem of change.* Boston, MA: Allyn & Bacon.

Szalacha, L. (2001). The sexual diversity climate of Massachusetts' secondary schools and the success of the Safe Schools Program for gay and lesbian students. Unpublished doctoral dissertation, Harvard University, Cambridge, MA.

Chapter 17

Some Challenges Facing Queer Youth Programs in Urban High Schools: Racial Segregation and Denormalizing Whiteness

Lance Trevor McCready

Relatively little is known about queer youth programs in urban schools and the unique challenges they face as a result of being housed in inner-city schools where the majority of students are poor, nonwhite and/or non–native English speakers. Here, I discuss my experiences working on a school-university collaborative action research project (CARP) at a California High School (CHS) located in a small urban community in the Bay Area of California.[1] My work on CARP led to independent participant observation of Project 10. This social/support group for lesbian, gay, bisexual, transgender, and questioning (LGBTQ) students was developed by Dr. Virginia Uribe in 1984, as a school-based dropout prevention program and later evolved into the school's GSA.[2] During the four years I worked on CARP, between 1996 and 2000, I became intrigued with the way the school's racially segregated academic and social environments affected student participation in extracurricular activities. As an out black, gay, male educator, I was drawn to the question of why, in a school where more than 60 percent of the students were nonwhite, Project 10 participants tended to be white female students. I conducted in-depth interviews with four openly gay, black male students, two of whom are quoted in this chapter. These interviews, coupled with my own participant observation in Project 10, led me to conclude that two important challenges face queer youth programs in urban schools: racial segregation and denormalizing whiteness.

RACIAL SEGREGATION

Like many Bay Area educators, I was initially attracted to CHS because of its racially diverse student body and extensive curriculum. Soon after I began working there, meeting and spending time with various faculty members and students, I learned that this famed diversity had a downside. Jerome Pettigew,[3] a black gay male English teacher, described CHS as "two schools under one roof." One school, he claimed, serves the needs of academically elite students who are predominantly white and Asian American (Chinese American and Japanese American) through extensive advance placement (AP) programs, extracurricular clubs and activities, and college preparatory classes. The other school serves lower-achieving students, who are predominantly black and Latino, with fewer programs to meet their academic and social needs. In short, persistent racial segregation in core and extracurricular programs continues to tarnish the otherwise hopeful integrated atmosphere of CHS.

While it was common knowledge that the football and basketball teams at CHS were predominantly black, I was less attentive to the student demographics of nonathletic extracurricular activities until Fran Thompson, the faculty adviser for Project 10, invited me to speak at a Project 10 meeting during the 1996-1997 academic year. On the day of the meeting, I walked into Fran's classroom expecting to see a collage of race and ethnicity. Instead of diversity, I found homogeneity: twelve white, female, lesbian and bisexual-identified students. So why didn't queer students of color attend Project 10 meetings at CHS?[4]

During the summer of 1996, CARP established the Taking Stock Committee (TSC) to investigate how CHS's racially segregated environment affects the academic performance of students, particularly low-achieving black and Latino students. Several participants in CARP suspected that segregated patterns of participation in academic and extracurricular programs created the impression that students' racial identities determined their level of academic success. Understanding how this link was created, we felt, was a first step toward undoing it.

Because data on racial segregation in extracurricular activities had not yet been formally documented, the TSC decided to survey faculty on the extracurricular activities for which they served as advisors. Questions included the racial and gender breakdown of students participating, target populations, recruitment strategies, and purposes of the activities. These data could not be obtained through traditional school records of attendance, discipline, or standardized tests. TSC also administered the survey through face-to-face interviews to increase the faculty advisor response rate.

Table 17.1, organized by type of club and racial composition, summarizes data on the extracurricular activities. Figure 17.1 represents racial demographic data by the number of activities that are racially mixed, predominantly students of color, or predominantly white. Immediately noticeable is the small number of activities that are mixed in terms of race. Of the seventy-three activities surveyed, only two (3 percent)—the Key Club, an activity that focuses on community service projects, and the boys' baseball team—were racially mixed.

Overall, extracurricular activities at CHS were racially segregated. Only twenty-two (the number of activities that are racially mixed plus the number of activities that are predominantly students of color), or 30 percent, were activities in which black students might see themselves represented in any significant numbers. Moreover, excluding those activities geared toward students from other nonblack racial/ethnic backgrounds, such as ESL Yearbook, Chicano-Latino Gradua-

TABLE 17.1. Extracurricular Activities Organized by Type and Racial Composition

Type of Club	Name of Club	Racial Composition
Academic/career	9th Grade Orientation B.E.S.T. [etc.]	Not available Predominantly white [etc.]
Athletic	Badminton Baseball (JV and VAR)—boys [etc.]	Predominantly students of color Mixed [etc.]
Cultural	African Students Association Chicano-Latino Graduation [etc.]	Predominantly students of color Predominantly students of color [etc.]
Performing and visual arts	Acting Workshop Baile Folklorico [etc.]	Predominantly white Predominantly students of color [etc.]
Social	Bubbles Club Star Trek Club	Predominantly white Predominantly white

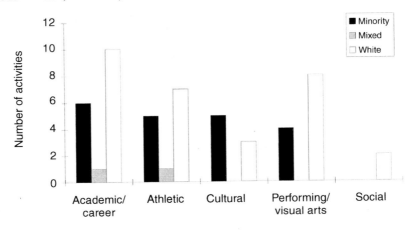

FIGURE 17.1. Taking Stock of Clubs and Activities, by Race

tion, and Vietnamese Students Association, only eight (11 percent) of the activities were ones where black students might interact with one another in any significant numbers.

Project 10 was one of the predominantly white extracurricular activities. Seeking an explanation, I interviewed two black gay male students, Jamal and David, who attended CHS between the years 1992 and 2000. Their narratives revealed how they felt themselves under surveillance by their heterosexual black peers who monitored the sexual "boundaries of blackness" (Cohen, 2001). For example, Jamal, who graduated from CHS in 1994, claimed that particularly among black students, to align oneself with Project 10 meant to invite unnecessary scrutiny. Jamal believed these dynamics were particularly evident when students read the daily bulletin announcing schoolwide events, including Project 10:

> [T]hey used to have announcements in the Bulletin, "Are you gay, bisexual, queer, questioning?" And then like I guess there would always be a designated reader for the class bulletin everyday. . . . [I]t was interesting because when I would have a predominantly white class in morning second period when the bulletin was read, like they would read it, they would read it. And people were just kinda like, just listen to it. There might be little side comments here and there, but they would listen and like, "That's a club in the school." But in the black classes that I

had, that same period? Ohhh my god, they would skip over it like the club did not exist. They would either speak through it [the announcement], or it was just treated differently than the other club announcements. . . . [T]here was a running joke at school like people wanted to go and actually see who actually went to the club. . . . [I]t probably stopped a lot of people from going, the thought of someone seeing them go. Like you don't want to be seen walking up to the third floor on the day that Project 10 is meeting.

Although Project 10 existed, as Jamal's memories suggest, it was not particularly safe or confidential.

Jamal's desire to display an appropriate black identity that maintained social ties with his black peers reflects what Signithia Fordham (1996) describes as the power of "fictive kinship." In studying the social identities and cultural frames of reference among black students at Capital High School in Washington, DC, Fordham observed that black students may or may not have been related by blood, but they maintained essential social relationships that served a political function as well. When black students used kinship terms such as "brother" or "sister" to refer to one another, it conveyed a sense of peoplehood or collective social identity. The fictive kinship systems of black students at Capital High School included strategies for protecting their identity and maintaining boundaries between themselves and white students. Black students perceived certain behaviors and certain activities or events as inappropriate because whites had established the performance criteria in those areas. Academic tasks and school-related activities represented one such area.

According to Fordham, since black students at Capital High were involved in the evaluation of group members' eligibility for membership in the fictive kinship system, they controlled the criteria used to judge one's worthiness for membership. The determination and control of the criteria for membership in the fictive kinship system are in contrast to those for earning grades in school. From Fordham's point of view, fictive kinship means a lot to Black students because they regard it as the ideal by which members of the group are judged.

"Fictive kinship" may partially explain why Jamal stayed away from Project 10. Based on more than five years of participant observation at CHS, I conclude that most peer groups, including those of black students, viewed heterosexuality as the ideal. Any black student daring to participate openly in Project 10 challenged this ideal. At CHS, identifying as black meant participating in extracurricular activities that were predominantly black and heterosexual.[5]

Heterosexist fictive kinship networks, however, were not the only reason why Jamal and other black gay male students avoided Project 10. Another invisible dynamic was the normalization of whiteness.

NORMALIZATION OF WHITENESS

David, an openly gay, black, biracial male student stayed away from Project 10 because the group's predominantly white, female composition alienated him:

D: [Project 10] is pretty much a select group of white girls. I've only been a few times. It's about four or five girls who all know each other. They're all out, you know, within that group. And they go there I guess for social support. That pretty much seems to be Project 10 at this point at CHS.

L: Has it always been that way?

D: Well, for one thing I think it's important to say that the people who are in Project 10 are all pretty close. I don't know if whether or not that's because Project 10 creates relationships or because they all knew each other before Project 10. . . . And friends of theirs who may or may not be straight-identified may drop in and just hang out with them. But usually it's not related to queer support. It's usually just a social place where I guess they can talk about their girlfriends or whatever. But, even then, the few times that I went they were talking about upcoming events as far as queer activism or a ski trip. . . . I went two consecutive weeks and then I stopped going because it wasn't doing anything for me. There's nothing there for me; right now it's just teatime for a few lesbians and their friends.

David's statement reflects the tendency of white female students, like their black peers, to socialize with one another around a distinct set of racially defined concerns, rather than build coalitions with students from different racial backgrounds, who may have an entirely different set of interests. In the racially segregated environment of

CHS, the lack of a social/support agenda regarding race seemed inadvertently to privilege those students who de-emphasized their racial identity. In fact, both the original Project 10 at Fairfax High School in Los Angeles and CHS Project 10 lack a clear purpose regarding issues of racial equity.

Virginia Uribe, a white female counselor at Fairfax High School, always recognized that queer youth were a diverse group. She wrote:

> Crossing every boundary of race, religion and class, they have sat through years of public school education in which their identities have been overlooked, denied, or abused. They have been quiet due to their own fear and sense of isolation, as well as the failure of their parents and adult gay men and women to be their advocates. The result has been a creation of a group of youngsters within our schools who are at significantly high risk of dropping out of school. (Uribe, 1995, p. 203)

However, she seemed less clear about how to address the needs of queer youth of color within the space of Project 10. Uribe implies that queer students of color should get their needs met by familiarizing themselves with resources in the community beyond the walls of school:

> The various cultures and races reflected in the United States are also reflected in the lesbian and gay population. Such adolescents face the prospect of living their lives within three rigidly defined and strongly independent communities: the lesbian and gay community, their ethnic or racial community, and the society at large. Each community fulfills basic needs which often would be imperiled if such communities would be visibly integrated. A common result is the constant effort to maintain a manner of living that keeps the three communities separate. This is a process that leads to increased isolation, depression, and anger, centered around the fear of being separated from all support systems, including the family. . . . As with parent issues, school personnel need to recognize the special issues that exist among minority lesbian and gays, and they should familiarize themselves with any community resources that may exist. (Uribe, 1995, p. 207)

By defining the complexities of identifying in society as queer and of color as a "special issue," Uribe, perhaps unconsciously, designated Project 10 at Fairfax High School as a space where whiteness was normalized. One could interpret her suggestion that school personnel familiarize themselves with community resources outside the school as an acknowledgment of the limitations of Project 10 to provide support for students with complex social/support needs. On the other hand, given that Fairfax High School is composed predominantly of students of color, to suggest that school personnel seek "community resources" for queer students suggests that Project 10's goals are politically narrow and deficient with regard to race.

Fran Thompson, faculty advisor for CHS Project 10, faced similar dilemmas trying to create and sustain a social/support group for queer youth that affirmed the identities of queer youth of color. Thompson suggested that the strong participation of white female students was related to the fact that they were the most concerned about encountering discrimination for being openly queer. In contrast, queer students of color seemed to relate more to groups outside of CHS, such as Lavender, a support group run by the lesbian and gay community center. Admitting that "Diversifying the ethnic composition of the group is very complicated," Fran questioned her own ability to comprehend fully the multitude of pressures that queer students of color face.

Like Uribe, Thompson's limited understanding of the social/support needs of queer youth of color may have unintentionally alienated these youth, encouraging them to seek resources outside the school. In this way, Project 10 and other queer youth programs privilege white students whose identities are viewed as normal and more understandable compared to queer youth of color.

DEVELOPING AN AWARENESS OF THE RELATIONSHIP BETWEEN CONTEXTS AND PARTICIPATION

American public schools are now twelve years into the process of continuous resegregation. The desegregation of black students, which increased continuously from the 1950s to the late 1980s, has now receded to levels not seen in three decades (Orfield, Eaton, and Harvard Project on School Desegregation, 1996).

The social context of urban schools has an impact on participation in queer youth programs. Yet too often the classroom or the club is viewed as island unto itself, independent of the social and cultural context of the school. Students and teachers who endeavor to establish and/or maintain urban queer youth programs that reflect the school's race and class diversity need to become aware of the social and cultural contexts of inner cities and the way these contexts affect participation in extracurricular activities.

CHS, like many high schools, is characterized by persistent racial segregation in academic and extracurricular programs. One of the most valuable outcomes of CARP was the positive awareness it brought to CHS faculty and staff regarding both formal and more casual belief systems and social practices that reproduce racial segregation in academic classes and extracurricular activities. When faculty, staff, students, parents, and administrators on TSC were given the opportunity to research the origins of racial segregation, they witnessed some of the social dynamics, such as "fictive kinship" that produces racial segregation. They, too, had an all-too-rare opportunity to reflect on how their practices (teaching, advising, counseling, etc.) might reinforce or could interrupt social boundaries defined by race, gender, class, and sexual identity.

Collaborative action research that is respectful of the knowledge that faculty, staff, and students bring to the table can open the door for more effective school reforms. Before starting a social/support program for queer youth in an urban school or when seeking to strengthen these programs, students and educators should consider investigating the social and cultural context of the school and surrounding community, and exploring how these contexts are having an impact on participation in school programs and activities.

DENORMALIZING WHITENESS

When Fran Thompson admitted that "Diversifying the ethnic composition of the group is very complicated," she questioned her ability to understand the multitude of pressures facing queer students of color. In doing so, she inadvertently normalized the lives of white queer students and relegated queer students of color to the margins of Project 10. Her narrative points to the need to denormalize the perceived whiteness of queer youth identity.

When whiteness continues to be viewed as the norm, even in institutions and communities such as CHS that are predominantly nonwhite, students of color are regarded as second-class citizens. When nonwhite racial identity is considered equally normal, queer youth programs are more likely to attract the participation of students from diverse backgrounds because the social, political, and support activities of the group are grounded in the concerns of multiple racial and ethnic communities.

More specifically, denormalizing whiteness creates opportunities for faculty advisors and queer youth advocates to diversify the curriculum of queer youth programs. Lipkin (1995, p. 351) notes that "if gay youth are exposed to the diversity of gay identities, to the richness of the culture, and to the long history of same-gender attraction, their development will be enhanced." Those who organize and/or facilitate queer youth programs can challenge the normalization of whiteness by making a conscious effort to use speakers bureaus and workshop facilitators that are racially diverse, decorating the meeting room with queer historical figures from multiple racial and ethnic backgrounds, and having books, magazines, and other reading materials on hand that reflect a range of racial and ethnic experiences about queer identity.

In addition, denormalizing whiteness creates opportunities for students, faculty advisors, and queer youth advocates in urban schools to build coalitions. Allying with other students and teachers who are broadly concerned with the ways multiple forms of oppression, such as institutional racism, poverty, and heterosexism, can make urban schools more effective and safe for all students.

For example, during the 1997-1998 academic year, David's frustration with the predominantly white female composition of Project 10 led him to organize a more diverse "political" group of students to fight not only homophobia and heterosexism but also racism, violence, and other forms of social oppression that typically intersect the lives of queer students of color. This new group successfully organized several forums on homophobia and heterosexism, including one aimed at students of color and another directed at teachers that made connections between the marginalization of students of color and the harassment of queer students.

After David graduated from CHS he became peer leader of a queer youth group housed in the city's Lesbian, Gay, Bisexual, Transgendered Community Services Center (LGBTCSC). During his tenure as peer leader, David succeeded in increasing the involvement of queer youth of color. To make the group more inviting to youth of color he organized dances and other social events that had a "mixed cultural flavor." For example, he made sure that dance parties had two dance floors that played different kinds of music such as hip-hop and salsa.

In addition to his work at the LGBTCSC, David began working with the newly formed GSA (that evolved from Project 10) at CHS. He coached the new faculty advisors (Fran "passed the torch" to two new faculty members in 1999) on how create to an environment that felt welcoming to students of color. He taught GSA peer leaders how to plan events that would appeal to racially diverse groups of students. In addition, David encouraged CHS students of color who were involved with the queer youth group at CSC to become more active at CHS. David's efforts with respect to antiracism work and diversity is a large reason why, when I attended a GSA meeting in 2001, the room was filled with a diverse group of CHS students that included African-American, white, Latino, and multiracial students.

David's work, which emphasized coalition building, antiracism, and a broad social justice agenda, is a strong indication that denormalizing whiteness can lead to stronger, more diverse social/support programs for queer youth that engage the entire school community in a war against the debilitating conditions of inner-city schools. In David's words,

> I think we're just fighting against something much larger. You know when you're dealing with issues of homophobia or you know racism or whatever, all the issues that people at this school have to go through day to day, I think its everyone's job to try and remedy these problems.

NOTES

1. CARP was a six-year project composed of collaborative inquiry teams of teachers, students, administrators, parents, professors, and graduate students who investigated the reasons behind two problems CHS has faced since it voluntarily desegregated over fifty years ago: the race-class academic achievement gap and racial segregation in academic and extracurricular programs.

2. During the 1997-1998 school year, Fran Thompson, faculty advisor for CHS Project 10, persuaded the group to change its name to the Gay-Straight Alliance as a way of connecting the group's civic engagement goals to a national network of GSAs working to make schools safe for queer students (Bass and Kaufman, 1996). In addition, Fran felt the name change would improve the group's demographics by increasing the number of heterosexual-identified students present at weekly meetings, which in turn would enable queer students to feel more comfortable being active in the group without "outing" themselves. From Fran's perspective, increased comfort with being openly queer could lead to a broader political agenda that included spreading awareness of homophobia and heterosexism.

3. The names of students and school personnel have been changed to protect their identities.

4. I use the term *queer* as an umbrella term for lesbian, gay, bisexual, transgendered, and anyone else who claims a nonnormative, nonheterosexual identity. I acknowledge that the term *queer* as an identity or statement of social location does not resonate with everyone. Besides the fact that the term *queer* erases certain sociocultural differences among lesbians, gay men, bisexuals, etc., some also consider the term derogatory. I currently use it, however, to acknowledge the limitless possibilities of one's sexual identity, rather than the misleading stability of sexual orientation terms such as *gay* and *lesbian* seem to imply. In addition, although most of the examples of queer people of color in this article used are black, I do not interpret "of color" as a code for black people.

5. The heterosexism of black peer groups and the resultant surveillance of nonheterosexual identities by "fictive kin" are often interpreted as meaning the culture of black people is more homophobic than that of whites. A full discussion of this issue is beyond the scope of this chapter. My sense, however, is that the idea of black hyperhomophobia ignores the question of how historical circumstances have led to varied expressions of homophobia in different racial, ethnic, and/or cultural communities. For example, Constantine-Simms (2001) notes that African Americans' expression of homophobia in the black Church is related to the ways nineteenth century missionaries in Africa pathologized the sexual expression of indigenous Africans. The present article implies that, in urban schools, it is worth exploring the relationship between black students' experience of racial segregation and other forms of marginalization, and the ways they express homophobia and heterosexism.

REFERENCES

Bass, E. and Kaufman, K. (1996). *Free your mind: The book for gay, lesbian, and bisexual youth—and their allies.* New York: HarperPerennial.

Cohen, C.J. (2001). *The boundries of blackness: AIDS and the breakdown of black politics.* Chicago: University of Chicago.

Constantine-Simms, D. (2001). *The greatest taboo: Homosexuality in Black communities.* Los Angeles, CA: Alyson Books.

Fordham, S. (1996). *Blacked out: Dilemmas of race, identity, and success at Capital High.* Chicago, IL: University of Chicago Press.

Lipkin, A. (1995). The case for a gay and lesbian curriculum. In G. Unks (Ed.), *The gay teen: Educational practice and theory for lesbian, gay and bisexual adolescents* (p. 351). New York: Routledge.

Orfield, G., Eaton, S., and Harvard Project on School Desegregation (1996). *Dismantling desegregation: The quiet reversal of* Brown v. Board of Education. New York: New Press.

Uribe, V. (1995). Project 10: A school-based outreach to gay and lesbian youth. In G. Unks (Ed.), *The gay teen: Educational practice and theory for lesbian, gay and bisexual adolescents* (pp. 203-210). New York: Routledge.

Index

Page numbers followed by the letter "t" indicate tables; those followed by the letter "f" indicate figures.